# Learning to
## *Soar!*

Escaping Rational
Captivity

Mark G. Becker

**BALBOA.**PRESS
A DIVISION OF HAY HOUSE

Balboa Press books may be ordered through booksellers or by contacting:

Balboa Press
A Division of Hay House
1663 Liberty Drive
Bloomington, IN 47403
www.balboapress.com
844-682-1282

Print information available on the last page.

ISBN: 978-1-9822-5533-6 (sc)
ISBN: 978-1-9822-5574-9 (hc)
ISBN: 978-1-9822-5558-9 (e)

Balboa Press rev. date:   02/08/2021

# Acknowledgments

Thanks first and foremost to my parents, Bernie and Ginny Becker. They were absolutely impeccable in their determination to love my sisters and me as well as they possibly could. I never saw either of them "take a break" from that commitment. No matter what anyone might say about how they lived or how they parented, there's no denying that the consciousness I live in today is built on foundations they laid for me in what and how they taught me when I was a child. Without those foundations, I might never have come to the mental and emotional space I am delighted to be living in now. I might not have arrived in the mind space from which I am writing this book.

This work is also an expression of an amazing legacy of additional gifts I have received along my life's path so far. Some were gifts from total strangers who had nothing to gain and would have suffered no negative consequences if they had chosen instead to ignore me completely. Still, for unknown reasons, they chose to reach out. Thanks to all those strangers, for gifts ranging from the simplest glance of acknowledgement, to real engagement in conversation, friendship, and companionship, however brief the encounters might have been. Other gifts were from family and friends who reached out to me in relationships that have been much more enduring and multi-faceted. For all of these relationships and gifts I am grateful.

In addition, of course, there were many professional teachers along the path of my formal education. Thanks especially to all who went beyond the basics to offer affirmation, encouragement, guidance, coaching, feedback, criticism, challenge, and even confrontation. I sometimes think of my life as a rope: strong but flexible, because it is made up of so many fibers. I know that every fiber came to me as a gift. There is no way I could thank all those important people individually, so I'll simply say, "You know who you are. Thank you!"

Thanks to all the other visionaries and teachers who invited me deeper down into myself and further out into the world, and who inspired me to hold fast to idealism, to always pick myself up and keep trying, and to never settle for anything less than absolutely everything. I've been privileged and fortunate enough to have known a few of these important people personally: Dick Harold, Jack Bartee, Henri Nouwen, Jon Das, David Kelsey, and Churchill Gibson.

Many of my most important teachers have been authors whom I never met in person, but their writings have served as foundations, pillars, and reference points in the development of my consciousness: Abraham Maslow, Rainer Maria Rilke, Steven Gaskin, Carlos Castaneda, Ram Das, Hermann Hesse, Robert Pirsig, Sorensen Kierkegaard, Scott Peck, Stephen Levine, Marlo Morgan, Daniel Quinn, E. F. Schumacher, Wayne Dyer, Richard Bach, Steven Covey, Rhonda Byrne, Helen Shucman, Bill Thetford, Mike Dooley, and Harry Palmer.

Thanks also to Roger Canfield, Lori Coburn, Paula Collins, Cat Songer, and Ed Stone, for their careful reads, early affirmations and encouragement, and excellent editorial suggestions, as well as their friendship!

Thanks finally and especially to my best friend, life partner, and Editor–in–Chief, Victoria Jordan Stone.

# Contents

# Introduction

*This book presents and explains a way of learning to understand and manage your consciousness intentionally, so that your default state of mind, most of the time, is as close as possible the ideal state of mind you most prefer. It includes actual examples from my own experience of discovering and learning to do this, as well as insights and suggestions intended to be helpful, should you choose to begin learning to manage your own consciousness more intentionally.*

If you're like most people, you live in two worlds. The first is mostly defined by seemingly undeniable realities like these (to name just a few):

- a job that's *OK,* but you wish it were better;
- the place you live, which is *pretty* good, but you wish it were different;
- a social circle that includes a *few* close friends, but no one you trust completely enough to fully relax into your deepest and most honest self;
- *occasional* experiences that are fun and entertaining, but they are less frequent in time and fewer in number than you'd like;

Unless you've given up, you probably live in a second world at least some of the time – an imaginary world in which many of those undeniable realities that seem to define and limit your normal daily life have all been transformed. This second world is your ideal – the place you go when you daydream and fantasize all the ways in which "life would be *so* much better *if only...*" In *that* world, you would feel more free and more fulfilled in every way. You would have all the wealth you need or want for living your life on the terms you most prefer. You would know with unwavering confidence – at all times and in all situations – that you are accepted and loved. There would be no more longing for a better reality. . . . no more "living small" and frequently lapsing into daydreams of *"if only."* You might think of that imaginary ideal world as your own personalized version of what organized religions refer to as "heaven." Unfortunately, no religion, philosophy, or any other body of teaching offers a guaranteed clear and direct path to anybody's version of heaven in the present. And if you're hoping you'll miraculously arrive in your heaven *after* your physical body dies, you may be out of luck there, too. There aren't any religions, philosophies, metaphysical systems, or new age constructs that offer rock-solid guarantees for that, either.

Being conscious, having a human body, and living a human life in the dimensions of time and space in the 21st century is an amazingly complex and dynamic experience. It can be a dazzling confusion of overlapping and often conflicting internal voices, expressing an endless variety of preferences, desires, regrets, accomplishments, failures, triumphs, frustrations, hopes, fears, ambitions, disappointments, gratifications, aspirations, and more. On top of all this internal noise, there's a loud and pervasive public discourse, full of information, advocacy, and entertainment. Most of this public discourse is thrust upon you, almost non-stop, by commercial advertising, which is constantly insisting that you spend your money on an endless variety of products and services, most of which have no potential to help you improve your experience of being conscious. Navigating in these turbulent seas is not easy, and no official handbook exists. Sometimes, the wall-to-wall complexity and intensity of it all probably feels like more than anyone could handle.

I believe some version of this is going on at some level inside most people's heads almost all the time.

If you've been working to overcome your version of this storm of interior noise and confusion, if you feel "stuck" and feel like you've *been* "stuck" for a long time, take heart! Prepare to see and feel things differently! Think of this book as a collection of observations, bits of advice, and practical hacks for navigating in the sea of consciousness. It's for people who . . .

- feel like they've been adrift for too long
- are tired of enduring -- or fighting their way through -- one intense challenge after another
- want to learn mental and emotional techniques that will enable them to travel forward in their lives more intentionally and effectively

This book is for you if you are ready to find and live into your ultimate paradise – your very own personal version of "heaven." It's "your very own," because it's unique to you and all the parts of your consciousness that are unique. It's "personal," because it's relaxed and comfortable, without all the serious and formal trappings that dominate descriptions of heaven in so many religious teachings. I want to help you find and live into whatever unique version of "heaven" has always been calling to you from the other side of "if only."

## Brief overview of the content

It's my hope that this book will be a fresh voice that can help you bring new order to whatever levels of frustration, confusion, and unanswerable questions you may have been experiencing up until now. It won't require you to learn and incorporate new knowledge, but it will urge you to learn a different way of playing the hand you've been dealt. Playing your hand differently will require learning to intentionally manage five aspects of your consciousness more effectively – beliefs, attention, imagination, decisions, and coping skills. You already have all five of those up and running on some level, using whatever you've learned along your path until now. No doubt, some of what you've learned is solid and reliable, and you know how to make it work well. Unfortunately, it's also quite likely that some of what you're "running on" is dysfunctional, i.e., not accurately consistent with the fundamental realities* of being human in time and space. If you're like many people, you have:

- beliefs that sometimes leave you feeling uncomfortable, dissatisfied, irritated, or in conflict with the realities of your situation
- habits of paying attention that waste some of your time and make a lot of the rest of it less satisfying than you'd like
- an imagination that is largely dormant; it only gives you occasional dribbles of enchantment, instead of the torrent of delights it's capable of delivering
- decision making skills that sometimes leave you feeling drained while delivering less than satisfying outcomes
- coping skills that, on the worst days, are barely robust enough to keep you moving forward

"Fundamental realities" are the bottom line generalizations that seem to hold true in all cultures and all times, no matter who you are or where you're from. For two reasons, I am respectfully avoiding any effort to name or articulate "fundamental realities." First, you most likely already have your own sense of what these are, even if you've never tried to articulate them to yourself or anyone else. *Those* ideas about "fundamental realities" are *your* starting point, regardless of how eloquent I might be in telling you about mine. Second, if you choose to work more seriously at managing your own consciousness, you may find that the "fundamental realities" you've been steering by are not actually so "fundamental" *or* "real" as you've been assuming.

If you're not already outrageously happy and delighted to be living the exact life you're in the middle of experiencing right now, the limitations are probably rooted in a consciousness that's running at least partially on "auto-pilot," somewhat out of sync with your context, and nowhere near as effective as it could be. If your current consciousness is not already delivering you into experiences of the personal version of the heaven you long for and dream about a lot of the time – if you're not already *soaring* — this book will at least provide some helpful options and hacks that are worth considering.

In the following pages, I've tried to bring five important aspects of your consciousness – beliefs, attention, imagination, decisions, and coping skills – into a focus that will give you a much clearer and much more accessible way of thinking about each one. I believe that as you develop clearer understanding of the role each plays in the quality of your experience of living, you'll be able to begin learning to manage each aspect more intentionally and effectively. That should enable you to imagine, create, and *live into* a much more comfortable and fulfilling version of your life than you have ever experienced before.

I've tried to make sure everything I've written has rational and empirical integrity. I've tried to describe and explain the patterns and dynamics I've observed in my own consciousness in words that will help you look inward toward your own experience and recognize your own version of what I'm describing. If I've succeeded in my intent, and if you take the time to simply examine your own experience of reality carefully, what I've written should come into sharp focus, and you should find all the correlation and confirmation you need.

I'm confident you can learn to manage your own consciousness in similar ways, and make similar adjustments to produce your own positive and beneficial effects. I don't know where you want to go, so I can't tell you how to get there, but I've wandered and traveled long enough and far enough that I'm pretty sure I can offer some strategic insights, useful tips, and navigational hacks that are worth considering. Wherever you are on your path, I've written this book to help you find your way a little sooner and a little easier to wherever you're trying to go!

## What this book is NOT:

- It doesn't try to offer a sure-fire final answer to anything. (It doesn't even pretend such an answer exists.)
- It's not a teaching book that will prescribe any particular path or step-by-step method for reaching any particular destination. It honors your freedom and your responsibility to decide on *your own* destination. It trusts *you* to choose *your own* path.
- It doesn't try to prove anything to anybody.
- It won't try to convince you that reality is *this* way, or *that* way, or *any* particular way. (In fact, I'm pretty sure there are as many realities as there are human beings.)

- It won't ask you to set aside time for regular practice in *yet another* new discipline. There are no mantras to chant, affirmations to repeat, DVD's to watch, or CD's to guide your meditation. (There aren't any on-line resources to consult or conferences to attend, either.)

- It's not trying to save the world, or you, or anyone else. As far as I can tell, those agendas are mostly dead on arrival. Personally, I've "been there and done that," too many times already, and life's too short to waste any more time allowing guilt or ego – yours *or* mine -- to take either of us on yet another side trip through those mostly unproductive feelings, motivations, and efforts.

This book is simply a smorgasbord of observations, insights, ideas, and helpful ways of thinking about the experience of consciousness, and the possibilities of learning to manage it intentionally. It includes lots of suggestions, and a few stories and examples from my own experience, but it's primarily intended to serve as a resource for your totally personal journey to wherever you want your life to go.

I've tried hard to avoid telling you *what* to believe or *how* to believe. I'm trying to make useful observations about the *processes* of believing, and how your belief system determines much of your experience. You already have your own unique consciousness. You're the only one responsible for what's in it, and no one should try to tell you what should or shouldn't be part of your consciousness unless you've *asked* for the advice. Picking up this book and giving it your attention is one way of "asking," but I'm not pretending to have your answer. I'm only trying to share some insights and suggestions that should be helpful in your process of finding your own answers. It's intended to help you manage the *processes* of your consciousness, but not the *content*.

I want to present what I've figured out and make it *available* for your consideration. However, I've tried to be careful not to *push* any of the ideas or advice you'll find in the pages ahead. (I've encountered my share of overly zealous religious proselytizers, knocking on my door at the most inconvenient times. While I try hard to respect their enthusiasm and good intentions, I feel psychologically violated when *any*one tries to tell me *what* to believe. That's especially true if I haven't asked for their advice. The feeling of an uninvited stranger stumbling around – *trespassing!* – inside my consciousness and daring to tell me what should or shouldn't be there is *not* an experience I would wish on anyone!)

Here are a few more points you might want to note before you begin:

1. Very little of what I've written is based on scientific investigation. In fact, cutting edge science is beginning to admit that it understands *very little* about consciousness, even though it's a phenomenon all humans – including scientists – experience deeply, powerfully, and intimately. It's true that I've successfully completed several college level science courses and I've read numerous books from both "hard" and "soft" science (biology, quantum physics, sociology, and psychology, to name a few.) No doubt, there are traces of rigorously academic science in my thinking. I have tremendous respect for science as an extremely useful tool when it's applied with appropriate discretion. But this book makes no pretense of being scientific.

2. If you have a particularly strong scientific orientation, you may need to "step out of it" – only temporarily of course – to

fully appreciate some of what you're about to read in the pages ahead. Don't worry. "Stepping outside" a purely scientific way of relating to the world is not intellectual heresy. You can go back to your scientific orientation whenever you encounter a question or problem for which science is the most appropriate methodology. Meanwhile, dabbling in other modes of knowing -- or simply allowing yourself to believe in a little magic -- may help you find your way to a more satisfying experience of reality!

3. You'll find no mention of Freud or "operant conditioning" – or any of the other scientific terms many of us learned from introductory psychology textbooks. I have used the terms "sub-conscious" and "ego" a few times, but in those cases, I'm confident that an average layman's anecdotal understanding of these terms will be sufficient. Scientific thinking and understanding of consciousness are peripheral to my intent. Rather, my assumption are these:

   a. Everyone experiences his or her own subjective version of "consciousness."

   b. Every person's experience of consciousness has multiple similarities to every other person's experience of it.

   c. There are some common challenges in learning to live an intentional life from within the limitations of a purely subjective experience of consciousness.

   d. A generally shared anecdotal understanding of consciousness, based on those subjectively experienced similarities, challenges, and dilemmas, is sufficient for a useful conversation about the possibilities of managing consciousness more intentionally and more effectively to deliver a much more satisfying experience of living.

# How this book is different from most other "self-help" books:

Since there are plenty of other writers and teachers already out there with similar intentions, it would be foolish for me to write yet another book repeating the same things they're already saying. Here are the ways I think this book is different:

1.  It doesn't require you to *"believe in"* any kind of god, healing entities, transcendent powers, exotic levels of reality, or parallel dimensions. It doesn't require you to develop any kind of "faith" in anything. In fact, if you're one of those people who mentally cringe when you hear someone talking seriously about "God," or "faith," or "prayer," take comfort in knowing this book was written *especially* for you.

2.  It doesn't require you to change your diet, get more exercise, chant, recite affirmations, or set aside special time for daily practice. It's more practical and immediate than any of those approaches.

3.  This approach is imminently *right-here, right-now, let's-do-this* practical. It's a functional response to the circumstances in which you've always been immersed. It's based on what you'll discover for yourself if you stop and take a good hard look at what goes on in your own mind.

4.  Learning to manage and fine-tune your consciousness intentionally as described in the pages ahead can begin to pay off almost immediately. As soon as you begin to practice the perspectives and strategies offered here, you should start to notice real improvements, no matter how "stuck" you might feel now, or how long you've been feeling stuck.

5.  Once you begin, it's simply a matter of practicing regularly and often. The best time and place to practice is in the midst of the normal daily activities you're already doing. No specially scheduled practice sessions are required, and there's no particular or minimum time commitment involved. If you choose to begin learning to manage your consciousness as suggested in the pages ahead, you'll quickly become familiar and comfortable with the processes, and you should begin to experience positive benefits almost immediately.

## Some thoughts on freedom

Some years ago, I posted a profile on an internet dating site. It included the following statement: "I'm serious only about living and loving as well as possible, by being as free as possible – free from inhibitions, self-judgment, guilt, fear, attachment, psychological baggage, and unnecessary cultural prescriptions." By "cultural prescriptions," I was referring to the fundamental assumptions, beliefs, and perspectives that are taught – both overtly and covertly – and subtly reinforced all around me much of the time. They are the navigational beacons that nearly everyone steers by as they do their best to move through their cultural contexts toward their ideal realities. After looking at some of the beacons I was steering by and after struggling with them for many years, I concluded that several were not helping me. In fact, I concluded that five of these assumptions, which had functioned for years as primary beacons in my life, seemed to be more effective at holding me back and/or keeping me lost than helping me get to where I was trying to go. Here are those five:

1.  There is a single objective reality outside and around me that has its own independent continuity.

2. The only responsible way to investigate that reality is through rigorous scientific methods.

3. It is unwise to give credibility to any explanation that cannot be scientifically validated.

4. The reality around me is absolutely impersonal; it is not responsive to me or anyone else in any way. (In fact, I grew up learning and believing in a reality that is neutral at best and maybe even hostile – or at least resistant – to any and all efforts I might make to develop my life into what I want it to be.)

5. To "make something of myself," i.e., to accomplish anything respectable or accumulate anything that has lasting value, I need to be extremely responsible and self-disciplined. I must work really hard, and even then, I'll need considerable luck to succeed at any significant level.

I was operating from within these beliefs, fully accepting them as unquestionable truth. These beliefs certainly seemed "rational," and in the world where I grew up, the only acceptable foundation for any respectable endeavor had to be rational, predictable, and safe. However, when I dared to question them and substitute other beliefs in their places, I discovered that none of these assumptions were consistent with the actual realities of human life in time and space. I discovered that together, they had been keeping me grounded and blocking my best efforts to learn to soar. By trial and error, I've managed to untangle myself (mostly) from their effects. Freeing myself from their limitations has been a large part of my escape from rational captivity. Here are the five core beliefs that I have established in their places:

1. There are as many realities as there are people, because every individual person creates his or her own unique reality (even if most don't realize that's what they're doing.)

2. There are multiple ways of investigating, learning, and knowing. Rationalism, simple empiricism, intuition, mysticism, spiritualism, and shamanism all served humanity quite well — for *thousands of centuries, in fact!* — prior to the development of the scientific method, which happened just a few centuries ago.

3. Science is not the be-all / end-all key to credibility that some would have you believe. In fact, when you limit your belief system to what can be scientifically validated, you are forced to leave out some of the most delightful possibilities of being human. Science will never be able to explain why you enjoy watching a glorious sunset or drinking a glass of fine wine. Would you really want to deny the reality of those experiences, just because science can't explain and validate your pleasures?

4. The reality around me is totally dynamic, flexible, and responsive to how I manage my consciousness. In fact, the law of attraction, as popularized by Rhonda Byrne in her 2005 book and video, *The Secret*, is increasingly supported by strong scientific evidence! In my experience, the clearest explanation of this evidence is by Dr. Joe Dispenza in his book, *Becoming Supernatural* (2019.)

5. The most important "self-disciplines, responsibilities, and hard work" are internal. My self-discipline and hard work are most powerful and most effective when I use them to *manage* my own consciousness *intentionally.* As I have learned to do that well, I have grown to experience more of the quality of life I most desire, including a nearly constant feeling that I'm living in my own personal version of heaven. Most of the time, I'm soaring!

# My qualifications to write this book

Most of the observations and possibilities you will encounter in the pages ahead began to occur in my mind only a few years ago. Since they began, I've been teaching myself to manage my own consciousness intentionally. What I've learned seems to be working exceptionally well. For me, it ha become an effective way of making real and steady progress toward the heaven I want, which is similar to what I believe other people want. I believe what I've been finding is the same as what many religions and philosophies advocate as the most desirable experiences of living. The more I live with and work with the ideas and perspectives described in the pages ahead, the more effective they seem.

It took me a long time to find my way to "here," and there were many dead-ends and detours — and a couple of complete "wipe-outs" — along the way. For nearly 40 years, I did my best to use rigorously rational and empirical intelligence to scrupulously examine and understand everything. I wanted to "figure it all out." (In my most private moments, I dared to assert that I wanted to be *wise*.) Creative use of rationalism and empiricism — with validation, reinforcement, and affirmation from hard science whenever possible — was my default strategy for trying to find the most intense versions of the best that life could offer. By the time I reached my early 60's, I quietly felt considerable pride that I had collected an impressive number of key insights. Unfortunately, I also had to admit that, despite my impressive collection of "keys," I still could not open more than a few of the most challenging existential and/or cultural "locks" that seemed to be keeping me imprisoned.

Then, when I was 62, I stumbled into a state of mind and being that still feels so good, I dare to believe I've found what all the fuss has been about when people talk about heaven, nirvana, perfect freedom, full abundance, soaring, flow states, and endless bliss. Even better, for you, is that I dare to believe I can explain how I got here in a way that might help you find your way to your own equally satisfying state of mind. What I've learned has become an effective way of making real and steady progress toward even more fulfilling experiences, which is not the same, but certainly *similar* to what I believe most other people want. It's about some new and different ways of seeing things and thinking about things that can help you learn to:

- Recognize and "unplug" the dysfunctional guidance you bought into when it was given by teachers you trusted at a time when you were young and vulnerable. (You had no way of knowing some of that guidance was *never* going to work for you the way they promised!)

- Become intentional and effective at fine-tuning your consciousness, so that it functions like a powerful radio. Instead of living in a consciousness that often seems to be a background of irritating static, i.e., the gray "fuzz" you hear when a radio is not effectively tuned to any particular station, you can learn to tune in any station you want, and hear it most of the time in perfect clarity. Instead of only occasionally stumbling across music you like, you can learn to tune in whatever kind of music you like best, loud and clear, nearly all the time!

The more I live with and work with the insights, observations, and concepts described in the pages ahead, the more effective they all seem. I've written this book in hopes that what I've learned can be effective for you, too.

## My hope for you, the reader

What you're about to read won't require you to buy into any religious, metaphysical, or new age belief system. It won't require you to even think about concepts such as "god," or "faith," and you won't be asked to stretch yourself to begin believing in any other esoteric new age woo-woo construct. My intent is to open your eyes to the possibility of playing your hand – exactly the cards you're holding now – a little differently, so you can "shoot the moon" in the best possible way, most of the time.

This book is my attempt to articulate the best of what I've learned and get it out there, where those who are interested can pick it up, take it in, consider it, and maybe begin to broaden, deepen, and intensify their enjoyment of being live. I believe this book can enable you to finally begin making *real* progress toward your own version of that heaven you've been imagining and longing for. I want this book to inspire you to consider the possibility of learning to manage your own consciousness much more intentionally and much more effectively than you ever imagined. I'm fully convinced it's possible for you to learn how to soar in your own life!

I hope you do!

# Rational Captivity

**To *Soar*:**

1. to rise or increase dramatically (as in position, value, or price); *stocks soared*
2. to ascend to a higher or more exalted level; *makes my spirits soar*
3. to rise to majestic stature

-- *Webster's online Dictionary*

When a bird leaves the ground to soar, it works at flying only long enough to find a thermal, i.e., a column of rising air. Then, it spreads its wings and rides that column of rising air to whatever altitude it seeks. From there, a soaring bird can travel for long distances and in almost any direction it wants, with almost no apparent effort. You might think of it as the aerial equivalent of surfing. Just as a surfer makes constant small adjustments to maintain his balance and his board's orientation in a wave, a soaring bird uses small muscles all over its body to make minor adjustments in the shapes and angles of its wings and tail, constantly adjusting its form in relation to the moving air. The water does most of the "work" to move the surfer, and the rising column of air does most of the "work" to lift the bird. But soaring is even more liberated than surfing, because a soaring bird is free to move vertically as well as horizontally, and free to travel laterally in any direction. A soaring bird is surfing on natural currents of moving air. You want to be able to surf on the natural currents that flow and swirl in your own life. You want to experience and live in that same kind of freedom: being able to fly as high as you wish and go as far as you wish, in any direction, with almost no effort. You want to *soar!*

Why is it so difficult to figure out how to *live really well, i.e., to soar in life*? If you're like most people, you see yourself as reasonably smart and self-disciplined, willing to do your best and trying hard to be respectful, pleasant, and grateful. Still, in spite of all your efforts, it seems like you repeatedly encounter limitations, obstacles, friction, resistance, confrontation, conflict, frustration, irritation, and sometimes failure. (On the worst days, your life just seems like "one damn thing after another.") No matter how hard you work at it, this pattern hardly ever seems to get any easier or any better. However, when you look around, you notice that there are at least a few people who seem to be improving steadily and "living much larger" than you are. You encounter their examples in books, magazines, and videos on the internet. Maybe you've even met and known one of these truly remarkable people in person. Some of these individuals even make their progress and successes look almost effortless. You ask yourself, "What do they *know* that I don't know? What do they *do* that I don't know how to do?"

If you've been searching for answers, you've probably read about the psychology of peak performance and "flow states," the spirituality of mystics, and the magical connections shamans supposedly have with nature. Perhaps you've repeatedly scanned the promotional materials for self-improvement resources, looking for *the* program that will finally give you the insights and answers that would enable you to transform your life experience. Maybe you've studied testimonials from people who have taken *this* particular course, or gone to *that* workshop with *that* guru, and experienced amazing transformations and improvements — people who have gone from "going nowhere with nothing happening in their lives" to making their wildest dreams come true repeatedly and consistently. They've gone from "dead on the ground" to *soaring*. You've probably thought to yourself, "If *some* people have learned to do it, there *must* be a way!" You quietly and desperately *want* that kind of transformation in your own life, but you've been trying so hard to make it happen for so long, that you're tired and discouraged. You've tried so many approaches with so little success, that you're now reluctant to speak about your most heartfelt hopes and dreams, even with those you love and trust the most. *Why is it so hard to learn how to live really well? Why is learning to soar in your life so difficult?*

I know how it feels to live these questions, year in and year out, without satisfying answers, because I lived in my own unanswered versions of these questions for almost 40 years. Fortunately, I began to realize there were shackles – both inside me and around me -- that were keeping me grounded. The more I learned to recognize and understand those constraints, the more I learned to escape. After so many years, and many discouraging failures, I've finally begun to experience the kind of significant improvements I had been longing for and seeking. I am learning to soar in my life!

# A word of warning

One of my editors has suggested that the remainder of this chapter is too dark, bleak, and negative. I agree that those descriptors apply, but I don't agree that it's "too much." Here's why: I believe there are both internal and external obstacles to soaring. Chapters 3-7 are about the internal obstacles, and fortunately, there is much you can do to free yourself from the limitations they impose. This chapter, however, is about the external obstacles. Unfortunately, there are many. It's also unfortunate that there's not much you can do to change any of them. Worse still, many of these external obstacles are so subtly embedded in normal daily living in 21st century civilizations, that most people hardly notice them. The best you can do is learn to recognize them, so you can avoid their limiting effects. Learning to see them may be not be pleasant, but there's no other way if you want to avoid them. Trying to soar when you can't see what's holding you down is like trying to steer your car in the dark with no headlights; if you can't see the obstacles clearly enough to consistently steer around them, you're almost certain to collide with them repeatedly, which will severely impede your progress.

So at this point, you have a clear choice: you can experience the remainder of this chapter as negative, dark, and discouraging, and you can allow it to feed pessimism, or even despair. ("If it's going to be this hard, why bother?") The much more enjoyable alternative is to take the rest of this chapter as justification for celebration and hope: there are a bunch of really good *reasons* your quest to learn how to live really well has seemed so difficult. You can give yourself a huge "pat on the back" for doing as well as you have in the face of so many subtle obstacles. And you can take heart in knowing that it's going to be a lot easier after you've learned to recognize more of the obstacles and manage their limiting effects in your life!

## Obstacles to soaring

In addition to my own flawed beliefs and assumptions described earlier in the Introduction, I have gradually leaned to recognize several significant obstacles in the environment around me. They are embedded in what I call the "public discourse." I will be using this term to speak about the sum total of all messages sent in the public domain. Specifically, the public discourse is composed of:

a) broadcast messages – graphics, sound, video, and text distributed by radio, television, smart phones, and internet

b) signage of all kinds, from ubiquitous small neon "Open" signs, to giant billboards in public spaces

c) print messages – hard copy text and graphics in books, magazines, newspapers, brochures, pamphlets, handbills, and direct mail marketing pieces of every shape and size

This huge flow of information is extremely intense and dynamic, saturated with millions of voices and messages. Public discourse messages are intended for the masses, or for sub-categories of the masses, but not for particular individuals (so the "public discourse" does not include the purely personal messages shared among individuals.) It makes no difference that a huge portion of these public messages are never actually given any careful consideration by most people. If they are sent, they are part of the public discourse. It's flowing in torrents, 24-7-365, and it's almost impossible to avoid.

Much of the content of public discourse is "what everyone is talking about." Some of the ever-changing content helps people stay connected with each other. It advises them about current events and their implications. It predicts what's likely to happen and dispenses advice on how to prepare. It analyzes what has already happened, and what those events mean. It's heavily laced with prescriptive and persuasive messages intended to steer both particular subsets of the population as well as the entire general public toward *this* path or *that* path forward. Your particular experience of the public discourse depends on how much you allow radio, television, internet, public signage, and print media to be part of your reality.

Some of the messages in the public discourse are helpful, informative, and entertaining. However, a significant majority are commercial in nature, and those are solely intended to influence the perspectives and priorities that dominate your purchasing decisions. They're insidiously invasive. If you carry and use a smart phone, listen to radio sometimes, watch a little television, and spend significant time on the internet, you're probably absorbing far more of these commercial messages than you realize. You might be amazed if you kept an accurate tally for just one day.

The public discourse is surprisingly difficult to ignore. You may *tell* yourself you're not paying any attention, but if a message appears within the scan of your consciousness, your brain immediately spends precious time and energy, analyzing and considering its potential value. Even if you decide to ignore it, the message has already stolen time and mental energy from your day. That was time and energy which you might have used for more authentic and more fulfilling purposes. Unless you make intentional choices to sometimes block out the public discourse entirely by turning off all your electronic media devices and/or spending significant interludes in nature (or parks where commercial signage is mostly prohibited,) you're essentially inundated by its messages, with very little interruption, much of the time. The constant mental load of assessing all these messages imposes a cumulative effect that can be more depleting than you realize. The public discourse can make it extremely difficult to hear yourself think. It can leave you struggling to become clearly aware of your inner guidance, i.e., your authentic preferences and ideas, and the vitally important visions and inspirations that arise from your deepest authentic self through your own imagination.

By my count, the public discourse contains at least five major categories of impediments to your efforts to learn how to soar in your life. Unless you make intentional efforts to keep yourself free of them — or at least take care to limit how much of them you allow in — these five can impose what I call "rational captivity" on your consciousness:

1. **Advertising** -- Unless you live a back-woods, off-the-grid life, you're constantly assaulted by an unsolicited deluge of commercial messages. At the risk of overstating the obvious, here is a brief inventory of the different forms of advertising most of us routinely endure:

   - **Video advertising.** This alone makes up an entire universe of dynamic messages, constantly blasting away at us, on an almost endless variety of "devices:" smart phones, tablets, laptops, desktops, wall-mounted giant screen televisions, and giant outdoor LED arrays making up huge "televisions" the size of an entire wall of a multi-story building. Even some self-service gas pumps now blare video advertising at you while you fill your tank. Most video advertising is in full color with full motion, in high definition, with narration and background music. This part of the public discourse is almost impossible to ignore. Several television stations such as Home Shopping Network stream product endorsements, demonstrations, and sales pitches, non-stop, with no entertainment content other than the "dazzle" of the products they are selling and the artful ways those products are demonstrated and displayed. Some of these "home shopping" programs are so seductive that people have become addicted to watching them and buying from them, sometimes racking up huge credit card debt to pay for products they had never thought of purchasing before they tuned in.

If you have any lingering doubt about the seductive power of video — regardless of the content being shown — make a short visit to your nearest big-box retailer of flat-screen televisions. There, you'll likely see an entire "wall" of the biggest and latest flat-screen models — some with screens as large as 6-7 feet — and most likely, they will all be displaying a loop of video intentionally designed to demonstrate their truly remarkable capacities for color, contrast, brightness, and clarity. Even with no sound, they can be so compelling visually that it's difficult to turn away. Many of them can now give you a visual experience that's more intense than anything else your eyes ever see, because their colors, brightness, contrast, and clarity are *beyond* anything you'll ever experience in the natural world, where nearly all light is reflected. Except for the sun, fire, lightning, and molten lava, only a tiny fraction of the things you see in nature actually *emit* light, and those few — lightning bugs, phosphorescent plankton, and a few bizarre deep sea creatures, to name a few— emit only the dimmest amounts of light in a very limited palette of colors. But nearly every tiny pixel in the visual field of a big-screen television is *emitting* light. The visual effect can be overwhelmingly compelling. It may even be addictive. (Note how many homes now have a television in every room, and how in some rooms, a big screen TV is the dominant element, almost as if it is some kind of altar.)

- **Audio advertising** – This also seems to be constantly blaring it's commercial "come-on's" nearly everywhere from a plethora of sources. Some radio stations market themselves by guaranteeing "at least X songs in a row commercial-free." The background music in retail establishments is often punctuated by commercial interruptions. Even when using your telephone, you can be subjected to a repeating loop of audio commercial messages while waiting on "hold" for a customer service representative.

- **Print and graphics advertising:** Wherever significant numbers of people pass by or congregate in public spaces, the visual environment is often thoroughly contaminated by a wide variety of print and graphic commercial messages. They're nearly everywhere, in nearly every form:
  - Photocopied handbills stapled to trees and utility poles, or taped to any available vertical surface
  - All sizes and shapes of signs on rigid posts or wire frames stuck in the ground
  - Business identification signs ranging from simple and hand-painted, to incredibly elaborate, featuring dazzling displays of light and color
  - Billboards so large they require permanent multi-story steel structures, just to hold them vertical and keep them stable through stiff winds. (And some of these monsters now display digital video!)

As you wait in the checkout line to pay for your groceries, racks of magazines and tabloid newspapers do their best to grab your attention with their sensational headlines and compelling full-color photographs. As you drive home, beautiful vistas of nature are contaminated by intrusive billboards. Even the sky over your favorite beach is sometimes filled with small airplanes flying "bumper-to-bumper," trailing banners advertising restaurants, golf courses, parasail rides, and shops selling beach apparel. Your non-digital mail is probably contaminated most days by at least one or more pieces of printed advertising, and some days, the advertising pieces far outnumber the occasional pieces that contain important information you truly need or want. My email inbox is also dominated most days by commercial messages I haven't asked for. Even when I delete them based on the subject line alone, they still suck time and attention from my day that I would rather have for more rewarding activities. (And "unsubscribing" sometimes seems only temporary at best.)

All of this advertising is being blasted at us, almost everywhere, nearly all the time, and most of us haven't requested any of it. Here's what makes this part of the public discourse such a problem: a careful look reveals that almost all of the content amounts to little more than modern day carnival huckster spiels, all designed, produced, and delivered in more sophisticated forms for today's more sophisticated audiences. Many are "pushing" the 21$^{st}$ century equivalents of "snake oil," with amazing promises about how much their products and services can enhance your life and improve your image. Most assure you that your life could be every bit as glamorous and attractive as the images they're showing you.

Many of today's commercial messages are carefully designed, and produced to convince you that your life will *feel* better, *look* better, and *be* better if you spend your money as they suggest. They can leave you feeling that, without their touted products and services, your life is "not quite good enough." And by omitting any kind of approval or affirmation of the life you're already living, they can leave you with subtle doubt that, if you're not buying and using their products and services, your life may not be completely acceptable. Such doubt can gnaw at your confidence so subtly that you don't even recognize it. You just feel it. Unfortunately, most advertising serves only the profit oriented motives of those who pay to have it produced and distributed into the public discourse. It's extremely rare to encounter an advertisement that even acknowledges, much less respects or supports, your authentic self and your desire to learn to live really well.

2. **News reporting** -- A second huge source of voices in the cacophony of the public discourse is "the news." There have always been newspapers, and news magazines, but now there's radio and television news as well. "Breaking news" is regularly reported at frequent intervals between entertainment programs on nearly all television and radio stations. Most broadcast news is regularly scheduled, but some stations are even devoted exclusively to news reporting all the time. In addition, there is an expanding plethora of independent sources reporting "the news" on the internet. Many of these sources supplement their factual reporting

with heavy doses – or entire programs -- of interpretation and analysis, followed by predictions about what will happen next. To compete for audience attention, nearly all of them resort to sharing stories that are increasingly sensational and graphic. Those "at the bottom of the heap," the least professional and least credible, resort to three primary tactics for gaining market share:

- making *whatever* they report seem important, or at least as sensational as possible (Check out the lyrics of the song, "Dirty Laundry," by Don Henley on his 1982 album, *I Can't Stand Still*.)
- overtly and intentionally undermining the credibility of all other sources
- presenting conspiracy theories as if they were factual

All of these strategies serve *their* interests, but not *yours*, especially if you're trying to learn to soar. The net effect of all this "news" is

- increasing horror about all that seems to be going on
- general erosion of trust in sources that, until recently, seemed stable and reliable, and helped people feel secure and safe
- polarization around more and more conspiracy theories, many of which are based on nothing more than hearsay, half-truths, distortions, and even pure fabrications that have no basis in any verifiable facts anywhere

The pre-defined intervals of news reporting also lead to problems. All kinds of events happen every day, but some days are actually relatively calm and stable; not much happens that's actually "news worthy." Nevertheless, if nothing truly newsworthy has happened on a given day, that doesn't matter to the people who produce news programs. The broadcast time has already been scheduled and reserved, and the advertisers have paid, so "the show must go on!" The producers, writers, and editors sift through whatever events *have* happened. They look for events that they can present to listeners and viewers *as if* those events were significant, serious, and/or important. They look for compelling visual images and sound bites. When necessary, they write and present relatively unimportant and largely irrelevant stories *as if* you *really* need to know about them. They use full motion color video, still photos, recorded sound bites, and carefully edited writing to make totally innocuous and irrelevant stories seem as dramatic and compelling as legitimately important news.

The next problem with radio and television news is that their stories are delivered by "reporters," whose performances are remarkably similar to those of professional actors. When these reporters are doing their jobs really well, they deliver each news item with voice inflections, facial expressions, and body language that are all carefully and intentionally orchestrated to reinforce the notion that, "This news is *serious* and you *really* need to know about it and understand its implications. You *really ought* to be concerned – maybe even *worried* about this news!" The reporters who do this most effectively become news "anchors." They are able to make the emotional part of their delivery so transparent that most viewers don't notice how much emotion – usually fear, or deeply serious concern – they are adding to the factual content of whatever they are saying. What they're actually doing is subtly manipulating your feelings. To be successful, a news anchor must be able to impart feelings of serious concern while maintaining a persona that is calmly and quietly trustworthy and reassuring.

The events at the center of a news story are nearly always dramatic. Stories that lack dramatic appeal are mostly ignored by the news media; those stories are simply not produced and served for your consumption. The events in the stories that *are* selected for production and broadcast may actually be inconsequential or irrelevant for you in the reality you most want to live in. Nevertheless, a successful news anchor rarely leaves you feeling that way. More often, the net effect of their deliberate manipulation is a nasty cocktail of dark and heavy feelings. They can leave you disturbed, saddened, or outraged by the *content* of the stories. You might experience mild guilt because you're not doing anything to help or remedy the situations described. And you can be left feeling hopeless because your capacity to render help is so limited.

Unless you experience the events in "the news" directly, you read about those events or hear about them through a *mediating* source. What you actually *experience* is your imagination as it creates in your mind a vicarious reality based on content that's been chosen and scripted by someone else. Psychologists tell us that our minds "learn" from vicarious experience almost as effectively as we learn from *actual* practice and experience. Your mind "learns," either way. Who wants to practice and learn – maybe even become an expert -- in experiencing *any* of the feelings you live through in reaction to horrific events in the news?

Here's yet another insidious dimension of getting your news from television and/or radio. With some stories, you'll decide fairly quickly that the news item you're watching or listening to at the moment isn't worth your time. Unfortunately, if you're like most people, you'll stay "tuned in" and suffer vicarious arousal of . . .

- fear ("Scientists report that global warming will end life as we know it by 2100 unless . . .")
- anger about injustice ("In spite of conclusive DNA evidence that Miller was wrongfully convicted, the judge has refused to grant a new hearing . . . ")
- despair ("After 17 years of war in Afghanistan, there's no end in sight as fighting between ethnic minorities escalated today . . .") or
- overwhelming hopelessness ("More than 600,000 refugees have been forced from their homes and now face starvation . . .")

Nevertheless, you endure all this and continue to watch and/or listen because the *next* article *might be* really important. You stay tuned in, because you have a vague sense that you might suffer negative consequences if you miss an "important" news item. To cope with that concern, you continue to subject yourself vicariously to the speaker's sense of fear and concern about what may actually be a story that has nothing to do with you or how you live your life. You lose sight of the fact that what you're hearing is not *the* truth; it's *just* a *story*. It's often irrelevant to your reality and so far removed from your daily life that you wouldn't be able to influence the events and dynamics described, even if you exerted your strongest efforts.

3. **Social media** – For most of us, Facebook was the beginning. Its original intent was constructive and creative: helping people to communicate with existing friends and find new compatible acquaintances. Unfortunately, it has become yet another platform from which commercial interests now launch still more advertisements. Facebook also became a broadcasting platform for anybody and everybody who wanted to say anything in a big way. It has become a platform for all sorts of audio, video, and print messages, cleverly disguised as news articles from reliable sources, when their actual intent is to manipulate your social or political perspective, or influence your purchasing decisions.

In recent years, other platforms such as Twitter have also proliferated, further intensifying the "noise" of public discourse. In fact, a shocking proportion of what is currently purveyed on social media is pure noise, neither truthful nor accurate. Some of it is intentionally misleading, because its purveyors have no purpose other than sowing mistrust, undermining credibility of authorities and trusted institutions, swaying your purchasing decisions, and/or fomenting social tension and political polarization. The result is unprecedented general levels of anxiety, tension, mistrust, and fear. The truly frightening aspect of how social media has been and continues to be co-opted by sometimes irresponsible commercial and political interests is that it is now being driven by AI (artificial intelligence.) For a much more detailed and eloquent description of what's going on "behind the scenes" of social media and the nefarious role AI is increasingly playing, watch the 2020 Netflix documentary, *The Social Dilemma.*

4.  **Guidance from institutionalized religion** — Big religious organizations are also significant contributors to the public discourse. To their credit, some of them have played powerful roles in keeping valuable wisdom and deep insight alive in times when despots and tyrants were doing their best to extinguish them. And I would argue that their voices in the public discourse would not have survived to the present if they did not contain at least a small mount of real substance that can be helpful to some people. Unfortunately, they tend to progressively wrap their nuggets of value in layer upon layer of distracting ritual and constrictive dogma. In some religious organizations, the original "truths" around which they formed have become so obscured, that their current teachings wind up enslaving more followers than they liberate.

    Unfortunately, even the best guidance from religious organizations can be quite vague and difficult to understand. Much of it refuses to digest easily using the usual processes of rational and empirical consideration. In addition, guidance from religious organizations often requires belief in transcendent "truths" and rituals that just don't seem to add up or make sense when you look carefully and practically at how the world around you actually seems to be operating. As if that weren't bad enough, the guidance and advice dispensed by these sources is often subtly contaminated by the personal and political agendas of the particular individuals dispensing the advice. Accusations of self-serving misrepresentation and hypocrisy are not without merit.

    Another downside of religious advice is that it often functions as a primary contributor to the development of a deeply personal sense of shame. When religious organizations and spiritual teachers make positive affirmations about the desirability of time-honored beliefs, attitudes, and ways of dealing with common situations and personal disciplines, they are performing a valuable service.

However, when they assert, as many large religious organizations and institutions do, that anyone who does not subscribe to their recommendations is less than worthy (i.e., "not good enough" as a human being,) or that such a person will suffer in some sort of "hell" after death, they are performing a destructive disservice. Such messages amount to psychological manipulation, pure and simple. They transform normal questions about existential uncertainty into nagging sources of unnecessary fear. They cause individuals to question their normal and healthy inclination to live authentically. They nudge people into neurotic resolve to become what they are "supposed to be" instead of what they were truly born to be. Soaring can only happen from within truly healthy authentic living. The cumulative effects of organized religions' participation in the public discourse can be antithetical to soaring

5. **The apparent pre-eminence of "science"** — It seems to me that the public discourse has an almost unquestioning faith and trust in the scientific method, scientific research, scientific technologies, and scientifically developed innovations, improvements, and solutions for major challenges and problems. This cult-like reverence for anything scientific is one of the most subtle but powerful forms of "rational captivity."

Don't get me wrong: Personally, I *love* science. I love how it helps us understand what's going on in both the physical and material world around us, and the interior world of thoughts and feelings. I love its power to help discover and reveal new and better ways of dealing with the challenges we encounter. I love many of the discoveries, technologies, and innovations it has already produced that make our lives simpler, more comfortable, and more convenient. I especially love how quantum physics and recent research on human brain function are increasingly validating ancient ideas and perspectives on consciousness, and the apparently unlimited possibilities of more fully utilizing our human brains.

In addition, I know and respect people who proudly think of themselves as "scientists," not because they earn their money doing scientific research, but because they claim science as their "home base." Science is their primary orientation in the world, and the primary foundation from which they consider and evaluate all possible ways of knowing, investigating, and thinking about reality. I am aware that many people think of themselves this way, and if you're one of those, let me assure you that I'm not suggesting your stance is wrong. However, I would ask that you consider the role of science in the public discourse with a slightly broader perspective than "normal." To did this, you will need to step outside your normal commitment to scientific thinking — temporarily, of course — but you will be able to return to it any time you wish. (And rest assured, "stepping outside" temporarily is not intellectual heresy!)

The public discourse almost never questions the role of science in 21ˢᵗ century societies. This seemingly blind faith is visibly pronounced in broadcast news: When news programs report on progress in science, you can often notice a subtle change in tone. Science news is reported as if there is some unspoken agreement among all the news providers that science will be reported with *true objectivity.* "There's no bias or editorial slant here, folks! This is *science!*" Or, "This is not just another news story; this is *new truth* that is absolutely 100% reliable, because it comes from *science!*"

Perhaps my perception of this preferential tone for "science news" comes from my own filters, from having grown up in the 1950's and early 1960's when science was still relatively innocent and trustworthy. It seemed ethical and honest, and the progress was fantastic. When Kennedy committed to putting a human on the moon by the end of the decade, no one in the world – literally, no one! -- knew how we would do that. We had to use the scientific method to systematically figure it all out, and after a dedicated ten-year national effort, we were successful! Back then, nearly everyone put science on a pedestal and gave it great respect. This is still going on today.

Sadly, even science is now sometimes subverted and co-opted by commercial interests. Through the 1960's and '70's, big tobacco companies spent millions of dollars funding studies to produce "scientific evidence" that using tobacco products is not harmful to your health. More recently, it has been revealed that big oil interests have known for many years about the dangers of fossil fuel emissions and the potentially devastating effects of greenhouse gasses on global climate systems and patterns. But "big oil" also funded studies to produce "scientific evidence" that there was no danger. Still, most mainstream news sources continue to show special respect for "science news." No other reality generating discipline gets this kind of preferential treatment. Religion certainly doesn't get it. Neither do philosophy, history, art, or any of the other humanities. Only *science* news gets this preferential treatment.

How did science become so inflated in the public discourse? Sometime in the early to mid-20th century, scientific methods began to produce frequent discoveries and innovations that seemed to make life easier. In fact, science began to seem like such a cornucopia of "miracle" breakthroughs that we put it on a pedestal and began to "worship" it as a new religion. In the 1960's, it was not uncommon to hear people say they "believed in science," or that they had "faith in science." Since science ascended to the status of a religion, and replaced religion in the minds of many of its most enthusiastic "believers," the public discourse almost never questions the pre-eminent role science seems to have claimed. This nearly-blind allegiance manifests in three significant ways:

a. Premature deployment of scientifically developed technological solutions; Too often, we have have failed to anticipate or recognize the new challenges — i.e., the sometimes far worse *problems* — that many "scientific improvements" have brought. (And shockingly, the scientific community still seems mostly oblivious to this reality.)

b. Extension of scientific thinking into areas of inquiry where it's use is actually counter-productive;

c. Over-indulgence and social pressure emphasizing and insisting on scientific thinking — and its derivatives, ultra-rational and ultra-intellectual thinking — in normal daily living;

First, regarding premature deployment of scientifically developed technological solutions, it's useful to note that prior to the beginning of the scientific revolution, numerous civilizations rose and fell over many centuries. Some left impressive ruins such as Stonehenge, the Great Pyramids, Angkor Wat, and Machu Picchu, which have endured for centuries. Others left barely enough traces for us to even detect they ever existed. However, none of those pre-science civilizations left poisonous scars that continued to fester and refused to heal long after the people moved on. In contrast, "modern" societies, through their hasty deployment of scientifically driven "solutions," have managed to inflict a considerable variety of wounds on the environment that show no sign of healing any time in the near future.

It's certainly true that the introduction of scientifically driven "solutions" has always been intended to make life safer, more convenient, more comfortable, and more secure. But while the intention has always been to "make life better," in many cases, and sometimes on shockingly large scales, our scientific "improvements" have actually caused new, larger, and more complicated problems. For example, the past two centuries have produced an amazing explosion of commercial and industrial development, fueled –literally—by scientifically developed technologies for dealing with oil. We use science to locate new deposits of raw crude, to develop new extraction methods (such as "fracking,") to refine it, to burn it, to develop exotic chemical compounds for industry and agribusiness, and to produce an almost endless variety of plastics. In the process, however, we have managed to contaminate oceans, rivers, and significant land areas with the residues of oil spills. We've saturated soils with cumulative residues of petroleum-based pesticides and herbicides, some of which have leached all the way down to the aquifers from which we once obtained drinking water. Runoff of these chemicals has contaminated lakes, rivers and oceans, damaging foundation layers of the flora and fauna in these aquatic environments. Some of these seemingly indestructible new compounds even concentrate upward in food chains, making it necessary to limit our consumption of several species of fish. We've contaminated most of the ocean floors with an almost universal "dusting" of toxic micro particles from decaying plastics. We've contaminated the earth's atmosphere with greenhouse gasses, primarily from burning fossil fuels.

The vast majority of scientists around the world now agree that those greenhouse gasses are causing global warming and disrupting world-wide climate patterns. They share a strong consensus about the disastrous long-term consequences of disrupting planetary climate systems on which all food production, and thus, life itself depends. Some of their warnings and predictions are so dark and bleak, that they invite anxiety, fear, despair and depression. At the very least, they arouse deep uncertainty about the future. For many, that alone has already inflicted severe damage on the accessibility of hope, confidence, and peace of mind.

With great help from science, we've been inflicting serious wounds on the environment, some of which may never heal. And we've been doing this at an accelerating rate for nearly 200 years. Yet even in the face of such obvious and overwhelming evidence, most people are still reluctant to acknowledge the potential downsides of enthusiastically anticipated scientific "improvements."

A second major problem with the role of science in the public discourse is over-extension of scientific thinking. People have become so enamored by the power of science that many have tried to apply it in areas of inquiry where it is not appropriate or effective. For example, when applied to existential questions, such as "Where was I before I was born, where will I be after I die, and what is the meaning of life while I'm alive?" scientific thinking fails to provide any meaningful answers. In fact, it does the opposite: it leads to doubt about the existence of any kind of life before birth or after death, and offers no answers about "meaning." (Some hard core scientists insist there is no scientific validity in the concept of "meaning." They insist, instead, that all of life will eventually be explained in terms of chemistry and physics.) Thus, the over-extension of scientific thinking, contributes to the rise of atheism, which undermines important pillars of religion, but offers nothing better to replace those pillars. Until the development of the scientific method, religion and spirituality had been, for many centuries, major sources of credible and comforting answers to existential questions.

Today, many religions are in decline. This is just one example of how the over-extension of scientific thinking has obscured, eclipsed, and even displaced other modes of knowing that served humanity quite successfully through thousands of centuries prior to the development of scientific methods.

Actually, there are at least seven distinct modes of knowing:

1. Rationalism – knowing based on simple observation, reasoning, and contemplation.

2. Empiricism – knowing based on direct experience. For example, if you've burned your hand on a hot stove, you've learned *empirically* not to touch a hot stove. That's *empirical* knowing. It doesn't require science. (In contrast, "science" can be thought of as "empiricism on steroids." In scientific "experiments," events and variables are carefully controlled to produce "experiences" in which relationships and causes can be more accurately identified and measured for sharper and clearer understanding and future predictive value.)

3. Authoritarianism – knowing based on directives from authorities telling you what to accept as "real" and what to believe as "true."

4. Intuition – knowing based largely on non-rational feelings.

5. Mysticism – knowing based on communications from a wide variety of transcendent sources of knowledge and power.

6. Spirituality – knowing based on relationship with a god, or pantheon of gods.

7. Shamanism – knowing based on deep connection and communication with spirit sources in nature

As stated earlier, these other ways of knowing guided human beings quite successfully for many centuries before the scientific method was developed. In fact, through the first 99.9% of human history, the scientific method and scientific thinking did not even exist in anyone's imagination. Whatever "certainty" people experienced was derived exclusively from other ways of knowing. *No one* knew *anything* scientifically. Nonetheless, humans not only survived, but thrived vigorously enough to populate nearly every environment on the planet!

Unfortunately, as a god, science can be harsh. If you give her too much power in your thinking, she does not tolerate dabbling in any other modes of inquiring, investigating, believing, or knowing. Thus, people who become overly intoxicated on science begin to believe that reality consists only of that which science can verify, or which science can easily study according to its own rules of investigation. Everything else is considered "subjective" and therefore, inappropriate for serious and responsible inquiry. Modern society's infatuation with science destructively undermines centuries of experiential wisdom, skills, and successes by leaving them outside the realm of scientifically acceptable reality.

Here's the third major problem with science: general over-indulgence in scientific thinking. This has led to the rise and prominence of ultra-rational and ultra-intellectual thinking and communicating in much of the public discourse, especially those parts dealing with government leadership and public policy. In early 21st century modern civilization, scientific thinking has so captivated the minds of so many people that, in many situations, giving credibility to any theory or explanation that can't be verified scientifically is considered intellectual heresy. When people come together to solve very real human problems, any possible explanation or solution that cannot be supported scientifically is usually dismissed with polite disdain. We seem to have completely forgotten the *thousands of centuries* through which human beings survived and thrived before anyone even *imagined the beginnings* of modern science. It may be that the importance of scientific thinking has become severely over-exaggerated to our own detriment.

This relatively recent flush of infatuation with scientific thinking — and the adoption of science-as-religion by so many adherents — has produced huge waves of public pressure for everyone to embrace ultra-rational and ultra-intellectual thinking and communicating as desirable norms for nearly all situations. It fails to recognize that, until the past few centuries, these modes of thinking and communicating were the province of only a small minority – priests, philosophers, and some members of the aristocracy. It also fails to recognize that the necessary mental capacity for this kind of thinking and communicating is not evenly distributed in the population. Some people's brains are simply not structured to be capable of it; these people process their mental and emotional content in other ways. Many more have the mental capacity, but some of them never received the necessary education to develop the skills. Still others have the mental capacity, received the necessary education, and learned the skills well enough to "pass," but never developed enough comfort with ultra-rational intellectual skills to use them regularly, especially not for organizing important personal priorities or making major life decisions.

Much of the public discourse consists of rigorously intellectually discussions of society's many pressing problems, and intellectually supported rational solutions. Much of it suggests that if we could just persuade enough people to see the problems through the correct rational and intellectual lenses, we could solve many of these problems. But an honest look around reveals that most average people in modern societies do not think or behave intellectually or rationally. They may be capable of it, but the important decisions in their lives, i.e., the decisions that collectively shape and determine the evolution of societies, are driven more by appetites and emotions: appetites for comfort, control, and convenience, and emotional loyalty to whatever patterns and priorities seem most familiar and comfortable, i.e., psychologically "safe." Most people prefer to live on psychological islands, surrounded by mistrust of anything new, unusual, or less comfortable than their familiar realities. When public efforts to solve public problems tolerate nothing less than ultra-rational and ultra-intellectual participation, they leave many people feeling marginalized, alienated, and disenfranchised.

Taking all these downsides into consideration, it may be more appropriate to regard scientific thinking, ultra-rational thinking, and ultra-intellectual communications, not as pinnacles of mental accomplishment, but as interesting mutations in human evolution. Nearly all life forms are driven to seek basic physical and biological necessities. At a less compelling level, nearly all life forms seek minimum acceptable levels of comfort, control, and convenience. This second statement is especially true of humans. If you look at patterns in the ways people in modern societies spend their time and money, you'll see that huge portions of their resources are devoted, either directly or indirectly, to pursuit of comfort, control, and convenience. Consumer-oriented economies are driven by endless consumption of goods and services that serve no real purpose; much of consumerism is little more than futile efforts to satisfy these appetites.

In most third world cultures that have so far avoided the dramatically transforming effects of western modernization, "enough" is still enough. (It's especially true in the handful of primitive societies in remote corners of the Amazon basin and remote islands of Indonesia and Malaysia. Some of those societies are so determined to avoid modern influence that they greet intruders from outside with violent aggression, sometimes even killing the intruders.) But in nearly all cultures that have welcomed and deeply embraced scientific thinking and are actively using its power to amplify their efforts to satisfy their appetites for comfort, control, and convenience, "enough" is no longer enough. The concept of "enough" has been eclipsed by an increasingly aggressive, arrogant, and never-satiated quest for "more."

The dynamic is remarkably similar to addiction. Nearly all addictions are progressive, leading to deterioration of the addict's judgment, which results in decisions that are progressively more self-destructive. No serious addict will easily agree to throttle back consumption of his substance of choice. Scientific thinking and it's extensions in the form of ultra-rational and ultra-intellectual thinking have been marvelously powerful and effective in helping humans "feed" these appetites (addictions?) for comfort, control, and convenience. If, however, our continuing use of these new modes of thinking and communicating to "feed our habit" causes us to progressively inflict irreversible damage on the life-sustaining capacity of the only home we have — Planet Earth — maybe these new modes of thinking are not so great as they seemed in the early periods of heady intoxication. Maybe a little moderation would be an improvement.

Still, shockingly few self-respecting intellectuals are willing to take any kind of questioning stance toward our cultural infatuation with science and the highly questionable prominence it has assumed in the public discourse. In the minds of many, daring to *question* the role of science would be almost unspeakable heresy. In fact, most scientists continue to insist that "more and better science" is the only reasonable way to deal with the problems we've already caused by premature deployment of scientifically developed technological solutions. Einstein said this about our efforts to solve problems: "No problem can be solved from the same level of consciousness that created it." Nevertheless, most 21st century "modern" civilizations only seem to continue rushing headlong into their unabated infatuation with science.

Let me reassure you (again) that I'm not *against* science. As stated earlier, I *love* science. I wholeheartedly acknowledge the many discoveries, innovations, technologies and solutions that science has produced to make our lives safer, healthier, more convenient, and more comfortable. I see and embrace the benefits. But I wish to point out that the public discourse seems almost universally unwilling to acknowledge the costs. I believe a healthy relationship with science requires that we be more cautious and judicious about when, where, how, and for what purposes we apply this most powerful — and potentially destructive — tool.

In summary, the emphasis on scientific thinking and its derivatives, ultra-rational and ultra- intellectual thinking, in the public discourse may actually be a confusing, divisive, and polarizing influence. There's still very little recognition of how much this emphasis marginalizes large segments of the general population. Nevertheless, much of the content filling the public discourse continues to be dominated by smug, self-congratulatory voices doing their best to convince everyone who is listening that legitimate, respectable thinking always follows two rules:

a.  Never believe in anything that cannot be validated scientifically.

b.  Make sure that whatever you believe and/or say is intellectually rigorous, i.e., not contaminated by any ideas or perspectives originating in intuition, mysticism, shamanism, or spirituality, but firmly grounded in socially acceptable, politically correct, well established "truth," and preferably, scientific truth. (It's almost as if science has become the only legitimate source of truth.)

47

Unfortunately, these two rules combine to produce a huge but extremely subtle social pressure that actually inhibits some people from thinking creatively about how to manage their lives. It discourages them from even considering other modes of knowing, and it limits the kinds of thoughts they dare to explore. This social pressure, so confidently served up by modern intellectuals, can actually inhibit or even block your ability to figure out how to live really well – how to soar in your life.

Over-indulgence in science is also insidiously complicit in one more unfortunate downside of advertising. Scientific research into the psychology of persuasion is frequently used to focus and refine advertising messages to amplify and intensify their effects. Thanks to scientific research into communication and the dynamics of persuasion, the level of insistence in today's advertising is more insidiously subtle and powerful than ever before. Those who are least capable of incisive critical thinking are the most vulnerable to being coerced by it and having their lives essentially hijacked by its seductive images and messages.

Those images and messages relentless insist that you will look better, feel better, and be a more acceptable and desirable human if you buy their products and use their services. Collectively, they fill your "supposed to be" image with so many requirements that people become consumed and exhausted in trying to buy-have-do-be all that is prescribed. There's not enough time in anyone's day to fulfill all those requirements, but advertising collectively insists that *we must* if we want to consider ourselves "successful." The challenge of trying to buy-have-do-be all that's prescribed leads to a frantic life, dominated by impossibly full schedules and endless days of being in a hurry to complete one activity, just so you can be in a hurry (again) to complete the next one. The drive to succeed, to fulfill all aspects of the ideals so heavily promoted by advertising, has left us with little time or personal energy for being patient, kind, understanding, and respectful in many of our dealings with each other. We're too busy. There's not enough time. The cultural imperative to be successful on this insane treadmill is probably a powerful contributor to broadly shared general anxiety and tension. Inevitable failure contributes to guilt, shame, and depression. No wonder depression and anxiety are rampant, and no wonder suicide rates are rising in all age levels, but especially among adolescents who are trying to figure out how to enter this "rat race."

No doubt, development of the scientific method is a pinnacle of evolution, (rivaled only, perhaps, by the invention of computers.). It is an extremely powerful tool. It can be used in support of creativity and life, but when applied without adequate forethought and consideration of potential long-term effects at both micro- and macro- systemic levels, scientific thinking can be equally powerful in causing unintended results that are even more problematic than the original problems they were intended to solve.

Until you examine it closely, the public discourse seems mostly rational and reasonable, even if a bit loud and intrusive. A closer look reveals how intensely it is contaminated by unhelpful voices and messages. They collectively and powerfully create widespread confusion and distraction. They make it a challenge to "figure it all out" enough to free yourself and learn to soar. For many, the distractions and seductions can be so overwhelming that escape is almost impossible. Hence the term, "rational captivity."

In the past few pages, I've made a considerable number of observations about what I think of as an invasive over-reach of scientific thinking, and its possible role in the public discourse. I'm not in any way trying to assert that my observations are unquestionably accurate or complete. However, in my own efforts to more deeply understand all that's going on, and further liberate myself to soar ever higher, I have found that these observations and perspectives bring the public discourse into a sharper focus that I have found extremely helpful. I only wish to share them for further consideration, and possibly, further development and elaboration.

In closing, please consider this: If you look around, you'll notice that nearly all young adults begin their adult lives with enthusiasm, zeal, and lots of energy for figuring out how to live their lives really well. Though they may not use the same words, nearly all young folks, as they enter their adult lives, entertain hopes and fantasies of learning to soar. Unfortunately, you'll also notice that in the face of rational captivity, few actually succeed. The majority throw themselves at the challenge for a few years, but gradually fall away, because the demands of "living the dream," as prescribed by the public discourse, consume all their intellectual and emotional energy. If those young adults have children and become parents, their lives take on additional responsibilities, making the task of "just getting by" even more challenging. For many adults in modern civilization, there's simply not enough time, money, emotional capacity, or intellectual energy left –after "earning a living" and "making a life" -- for any continuing efforts to learn how to *live really well*. Conveniently, advertising often advocates a self-serving remedy for this problem, too: it portrays "success," not as figuring out how to soar, but as earning and accumulating enough money to give yourself so many privileges, comforts, indulgences, and distractions (i.e., so much mental and emotional anesthesia,) that you can comfortably and permanently *abandon* the goal of learning to live intensely, learning to soar. In the words of Pink Floyd:

"The child is grown

The dream is gone

I have become comfortably numb."

> *- From their song, "Comfortably Numb," on* The Wall, *(1979)*

If you've been tempted to give up, don't despair. There are legitimate reasons it has been so difficult. But it's not impossible, and leaning to soar is not so "out of reach" as you might have concluded. This book is an attempt to offer fresh help. As stated in the Introduction, the content is based on simple observations you can confirm by looking carefully at your own experiences. And the suggestions offered won't require any expenditure of time or money that you're not already spending. Escaping rational captivity and learning to soar is mostly a matter of developing some different disciplines and habits in how you manage your beliefs (Chapter 2,) spend your attention and time (Chapter 3,) and use your imagination (Chapter 4.)

It's never too late to give it another try, and learning to soar is well worth the extra effort!

# Beliefs

*Managing your system of beliefs is*
*the first step in learning to soar.*

My first exposure to the idea that "your belief system determines your reality" occurred 10-15 years ago. I intuitively recognized some truth in the assertion, but I had no idea exactly how to understand it clearly or explain the concept in detail. Harry Palmer's book *Living Deliberately* (1994 and subsequent) was a big help to me in developing the mental constructs of a much more detailed and articulate understanding. My 2017 participation in the first courses of Palmer's Avatar training materials was also instrumental, although what you will find in the pages ahead has diverged considerably from his way of conceptualizing and working with beliefs systems.

Long before I encountered Harry Palmer, I had already tried to categorize everything that goes on at the deepest levels of my consciousness. I had identified nine categories: *(The accompanying definitions are primarily from Google.)*

1.  Attitudes – These make up your repertoire of default emotional states, from which you tend to react (unless you intentionally choose a different emotional space.) To a large degree, attitudes are combinations of assumptions and expectations,

2.  Assumptions – The realities you accept as true without needing any kind of proof or validation. These are similar to beliefs, except they tend to be less deeply entrenched and more amenable to modification or substitution.

3. Beliefs – A "belief" is acceptance that a statement is true, or that something exists. Here are a couple of examples: "Accomplishing anything worthwhile always requires hard work." "Being willing to work hard is a desirable attribute." Google's second definition is, "Trust, faith, or confidence in someone or something," and the example is, "a belief in democratic politics." Beliefs are very similar to assumptions except that they tend to have continuity and stability over longer periods of time. They are more deeply entrenched, and less amenable to change.

4. Perspectives – A perspective is a particular attitude toward (or way of regarding) something; a perspective is a point of view. "Most history is written from the editor's perspective." Here's a second definition: "True understanding of the relative importance of things; a sense of proportion." (The words, "relative importance" imply an organizational scheme with some kind of hierarchy of elements.)

5. Values – A value is the regard that something is held to deserve; the importance, worth, or usefulness of something; also, a person's principles or standards of behavior; one's judgment of what is *important* in life, i.e., likely to have a profound effect on success, survival, or well-being.

6. Expectations – Strong beliefs that particular events will happen or become real in the future. "Reality had not lived up to expectations." On the personal level, an expectation is a belief that someone will or should achieve something.

7. Hopes – Wanting a certain thing to happen. Hopes are less certain than expectations, but tend to be more positively oriented. Dread and worry are negative and counter-productive forms of hoping.

8. Fears – Unpleasant emotions caused by a belief that someone or something is dangerous, destructive, likely to cause pain, or likely to become a threat.

9. Attachments – An attachment is a feeling that there is an important connection or continuity between yourself and some particular person, object, idea, concept, or value. The word usually implies strong resistance to any factor that threatens the continuity or validity of the perceived connection.

Obviously, there is some overlap among these definitions, but establishing fine distinctions between the labels is not nearly so important as recognizing the dynamics these generate in your consciousness. Collectively, they greatly determine the quality and feeling of your experience of being alive. (*NOTE:* From here on, the word "beliefs" will refer to *any kind of mental activity that would be an example from any of these nine categories.*)

This system of nine categories has remained remarkably stable in my experience. Many times, I've challenged myself to identify an element of mental activity that wouldn't fit into one or another of these categories, but so far, I have not been able to find a single example that's not addressed by this system. Of course, your consciousness is never limited to these categories. It's always processing — making plans, participating in conversations, visualizing the future, remembering the past, developing strategies for achieving or acquiring, guiding accomplishment of tasks in the physical world, or vicariously experiencing the script for a reality that was imagined and packaged for your consumption by people far removed from your current situation. Meanwhile, all the beliefs in these nine categories operate continuously like default settings, or lines of code in a computer operating system. Just as the operating system determines how a computer manages a software application, these nine aspects of your consciousness – attitudes assumptions, beliefs, perspectives, values, expectation, hopes fear and attachments – are always influencing how you approach and how you experience all the other activities and thought processes that occupy your mind.

I had been using this set of categories in my own thinking for more than ten years before I noticed that each of these aspects of consciousness is entirely subjective. Psychologists may do their best to study each of them "scientifically," but there's no aspect of any of them that can be scientifically measured directly. Psychological experiments can only measure and count *indicators* – not the actual realities of an attitude, assumption, belief or perspective. In fact, science has no way to *directly* measure any of the foundations upon which consciousness is built. (This is good example of how "scientific knowing" is not possible for some of the most fundamental and important aspects of being human, i.e., experiencing consciousness.)

Most people have little or no awareness of their belief systems. Imagine a fish that has never known anything *other* than being completely *surrounded by* and *suspended in* water. That fish cannot possibly have any perspective on water, because the presence of water has been part of every moment of its awareness for its entire life. The fish has no way to distinguish water from any background, because for the fish, water *is* and *always has been* the *only* background it has ever known. For a fish, "water" and "background" are the same thing. For most people, the existence of a belief system and its impact on consciousness is similar. It's background that seems invisible, because it's been there every waking moment since your consciousness began to develop. It doesn't even seem to exist until you look carefully. Nevertheless, your belief system is an important part of the sorting mechanism that determines which sensory inputs will be delivered to your conscious awareness, and which ones will be ignored.

Once new information arrives in your brain, your belief system determines how it will be perceived. However, even before new information arrives in your waking awareness, a part of your brain, the amygdala, examines each new bit to address survival questions such as these: "Is this harmful, or is it helpful? Is this important, or not important? If it's important, how important is it? Is it important enough to adjust my understanding of who I am and change my way of operating in this and all similar future situations?" Every iota of information that arrives in your brain goes through this kind of analysis, and some of your unique ways of analyzing are based on your belief system. This process is happening every waking moment. It happens so quickly that you're not even aware of it. Yet, it largely determines who you are and how you perceive your life at every moment. If you want the experience of your life to evolve to feel more like your own personal version of heaven, you must become aware of your belief system, understand how it operates, and learn to fine-tune it intentionally.

Here's how deeply and completely your beliefs determine your reality. If you had been raised in a dramatically different culture halfway around the world – for example, if your biological parents were western Europeans, but they gave you up for adoption at infancy and you were adopted and raised by Chinese parents and care providers in a purely Chinese setting – you would have a very different belief structure from your western European biological parents. You would have the DNA and all the *physical* attributes of a western European, but essentially, you would *be* Chinese because your belief system would be entirely based on beliefs derived from Chinese culture.

Differences in belief systems are what make international travel and visiting foreign cultures so fascinating. When you visit a culture that is foreign, i.e., different from the culture in which your own belief system was formed, you *see* and *experience directly* the different realities generated by people who share a different belief system. Such differences produce different art, architecture, language, music, food, fashion, etc. A different *belief system* generates a different *culture*. This is the essence of what you're referring to when you speak of "a different culture."

## One reason self-help books often fail to produce desired results:

Everyone has a system of beliefs that serves as the foundation of his or her consciousness. A system is a composed of three or more related parts which, together, form a complex whole. The cumulative effect on the whole is always a function of the *interactions* among the parts. Whatever you experience in your awareness is always a function of the collective effects of all the attitudes, assumptions, beliefs, perspectives, values, expectations, hopes, fears, and attachments that are involved at the time. Your beliefs dramatically influence both *what* you notice and *how* you perceive it in any situation. Therefore, your belief system greatly determines your experience of reality.

Your belief system operates in your consciousness the same way a computer's operating system determines how it handles any software application you might try to load and run. A single error in a single line of code in a computer's operating system can severely limit or even completely block that computer's capacity to run software. If it runs at all, it's unlikely to run well until corrections are made. A *dysfunctional* belief is one that is out of sync with the fundamental realities of human life in time and space. It's the biological equivalent of 'bad code" in the "operating system" of your consciousness. It inhibits or blocks your capacity to accurately perceive what's going on. If you can't perceive accurately, you can't relate effectively. In pursuit of your ideal life, you can make all sorts of investments in "personal development" software applications. You can read the latest self-help books, listen to the best CD's, watch the very best videos. You can pay big money to sit at the feet of the latest gurus of spirituality, self-actualization, or success in business. But if you have dysfunctional beliefs still lurking in your "operating system," none of those "best programs" will "run" as effectively as they should. At best, you'll see only modest results from even your most determined efforts.

This is a major fallacy of many self-help resources: *they fail to address the limitations imposed by dysfunctional elements in a person's belief system.* Until your belief system is cleaned up and running smoothly, i.e., in perfect harmony with the fundamental realities of human living in time and space, the reality you most want to experience – being able to soar into your own unique version of heaven – will remain largely inaccessible, no matter what strategies and resources you use, and no matter how much self-discipline you apply or effort you make.

## Where and how did your belief system originate?

Assume with me for a moment that when you came into the world as an infant, your consciousness was like a blank hard drive in a computer. A person who believes in reincarnation may react to this opening assumption by asserting a belief that previous incarnations can *also* contribute to the content of a person's belief system in the current lifetime. But notice: *that* belief would not make sense without a *prior* belief that reincarnation itself is a real phenomenon. Is reincarnation real? For those who *believe* it is real, it most certainly *is* "real" in the reality they experience. For those who don't believe in reincarnation, it's *not* "real." Both beliefs are real, both are true, and each belief leads to its own legitimate reality. That's the way beliefs operate. (This is just one example which illustrates why it's important to recognize how powerfully beliefs determine reality!)

Continuing from the original assumption, it makes sense to imagine that at the moment of your birth, no operating system had been loaded onto your hard drive, and none of the beliefs that eventually made up the earliest version of your belief system had been formed. You absorbed your initial belief system from your primary care-givers. Their biological relationship to you made no difference at all. They might have been parents, grandparents, brothers, sisters, an aunt or an uncle or a neighbor from down the street who took care of you a lot of the time while your Mom and Dad were busy earning a living. In all of the time your caregivers were feeding you, clothing you, and keeping you clean, they were inadvertently projecting themselves – including whatever dysfunctional beliefs were still lurking in *their* operating systems – into you. They probably had little or no awareness that this was happening, so in most cases, it would be a stretch to say this process was intentional. Just by making you the focus of their attention, they were making you real in their own perception, and in the process, they were *imprinting you* with the beliefs from which *they* were living. Being completely innocent and vulnerable, you inevitably absorbed at least some of their dysfunctional beliefs.

As soon as you began to acquire language, your care givers began to intentionally define and develop your belief system. Their efforts took on dramatic new levels of power, because language enabled them to "copy their belief files" more *directly* into you. They began to give you direct instructions about attitudes, assumptions, values, etc. to include in your belief system: "It's not nice to hit, we don't do that." "You must share your toys." "Never accept candy from strangers." No doubt, they were teaching you the best they knew with every good intention, but unless they were all working from highly refined belief systems, you inevitably absorbed at least a few more of their dysfunctional beliefs as well, such as these: "People in this family don't go to college." or, "It's wrong to question authority" or "It's not OK to associate with people who are not like us." This process happened much more quickly and powerfully after you began to develop language skills. Unless you've already done the work to clean up and fine tune your belief system, whatever beliefs you absorbed are still operating and exerting strong influence –sometimes imposing significant limitations – on how you see yourself, how you operate in the world, what you have made of yourself so far, and what you can become in the future. What you are actually *capable* of becoming or achieving may be severely limited by what you *believe* you can become or achieve.

Here's one possible example of how dysfunctional beliefs can be instilled in a child: many children are taught from a very early age some form of the following: "It's important to conduct yourself so that people will like you." While it's certainly preferable for people to perceive you positively, it's even more important that you learn to conduct yourself so that *you* will like *yourself.* If this kind of guidance was given to you without balancing messages, i.e., regular and healthy affirmations of the unique and/or unusual qualities that make you different from everyone else, you may have inadvertently learned to believe your uniqueness was not important. You may have learned to ignore large parts of your authentic self, or even to suppress it so much that you've lost touch with it. Being out of touch with your authentic unique self is no basis for optimal mental health, and makes learning to soar far more difficult. When you were a child, you were innocent and vulnerable, so you probably took in most of the advice and guidance you were given without recognizing its limitations. Unfortunately, if left unexamined, such flawed advice can endure as ongoing, second-nature, default beliefs, even though they are dysfunctional and counterproductive.

I'm not a trained psychologist, and I'm not pretending to be, but I suspect that development of ego in a child is largely fueled by guidance and advice from adult care providers. When a mother reacts to a selfish behavior in her son by counseling, "Nice boys don't do that, and we want you to be a nice boy," she is encouraging her son to imagine an ideal and preferred reality called "nice boy." She is giving some definition to what a "nice boy" is and is not, and encouraging her son to bend his natural authentic behaviors toward his developing mental image of a "nice boy." Through this kind of guidance, a child gradually builds up a comprehensive internal image of what he or she is "supposed to be." Even if affirmations of authentic uniqueness are also given in equal measure – in contrast to the example above – much of the advice and guidance the child receives will encourage further development of this internalized image of what the self is "supposed to be." Failure to act consistently with an imagined version of ideal self – as described above – can also elicit negative feedback that encourages a person to perceive his or her authentic responses and inclinations as problematic.

If a child discovers that acting – i.e., "acting" in much the same way a professional stage actor "acts" — as s/he is "supposed to act" results in the richest and most satisfying positive reinforcement, the child is likely to develop a sense that acting from this imagined version of self, with all its prescriptions and taboos, is a more successful strategy for gaining approval and securing nurture than acting authentically. From that point on, living through this imagined version of self becomes an important strategy in the child's life. This is a reasonable way to think about how ego begins. As a child matures, s/he sees that the flow of societal rewards is a direct function of how well s/he can live into and through this socially preferred self, even though it is entirely imaginary. Protecting and defending the reputation of this imagined self becomes increasingly important. Eventually, this imagined ideal self can so totally eclipse the authentic self that a person can lose connection with their ability to act authentically, except in rare circumstances such as crisis. S/he may even completely lose touch with authentic personal identity.

Failure to act consistently with an imagined version of ideal self – as described above – can also elicit negative feedback that encourages a person to perceive his or her most authentic responses and inclinations as problematic. This is one of the origins of "I'm not good enough," a belief that persistently oppresses many individuals — even adults — and quietly haunts many more.

Following these early years in which beliefs are instilled almost exclusively by primary care givers, almost every child goes through some kind of formal educational process. In modern western civilizations, this is usually some form of public or private school, rather than the less formal processes of indigenous cultures. Formal education is usually served up by an entire institution, staffed by well-meaning professionals. The purpose of these institutions is to "educate" you, but that purpose could also be also be stated as "impose a massively comprehensive and systematic agenda of programming on your consciousness." Inevitably, that includes beliefs, especially if you were regularly involved with any kind of religious organizations, most of which are heavily invested in promoting beliefs. Beliefs are embedded in decisions about how most academic subjects will be taught. For example, in history, beliefs determine which stories will be told, as well as the perspective from which they'll be told. Do you really suppose that German textbooks on 20th century history tell the story of World War II the same way American textbooks tell it? Beliefs about how people *ought* to govern themselves are deeply embedded in every civics course. The "great works" of literature endure through the centuries because they express enduring beliefs about the best ways to deal with the dynamics and logistics of life and its existential enigmas. Even the most academically "pure" curriculum will inevitably include beliefs.

Your education system probably also attempted to fill your memory banks with "background data" that had been selected and approved by the same officials who made all the other decisions about the content their system would teach. Their intention was to impart information that would equip you for tasks and decisions they believed you would face later in life. They did their best to fill your mind with what they considered to be the most generally effective vocabulary and understanding of the culture, as well as skills for effective thinking, problem solving, planning, coping, and appropriate self-management within your culture. It would be almost impossible to design a curriculum for teaching all this without inadvertently promoting some beliefs as being more advantageous than others. Although it may sound harsh, it would not be completely inaccurate to say that the belief system that was dominant in the development of your school's entire curriculum was *inflicted* on you. This was done with the best of intentions, of course. But it's highly unlikely that you survived it without absorbing at least a few *more* beliefs that are actually dysfunctional in your current reality.

In more modern cultures, the process of shaping and developing a young person's belief system usually continues well beyond the physiological changes that mark the beginning of adolescence. But since we are somewhat "hardwired" by thousands of generations – it's in our genes – to have completed our belief system development by the beginning of adolescence, continuing efforts by the surrounding system to further shape and program a person's beliefs often encounter resistance. In modern western civilizations, this resistance is commonly known as "adolescent rebellion." If a child has been successfully taught a belief that questioning or resisting authority is inappropriate, that child may remain compliant and obedient, dutifully subordinating himself or herself to continued development and programming by the belief-instilling agencies of the culture.

However, if that belief has not been firmly established, most healthy young individuals will probably begin feeling and saying, sometime in early adolescence, some version of the following: "I'm tired of listening to grownups tell me how to do everything. I want to do it on my own now." This attitude usually grows and intensifies gradually. It eventually transforms into some version of this statement: "Enough! I'm in charge, now. I'll do it my own way from now on." If this happens relatively early after the onset of adolescence, the child may "drop out" of the culturally preferred educational processes and turn to whatever employment opportunities s/he can find to begin making an adult life. However, if this normal and healthy urge to begin managing one's self without external guidance is adequately suppressed, a person may continue to allow religious organizations, institutions of higher learning, professional societies, or other sources of programming such as political and military organizations to further shape and determine his or her belief system.

This whole process of beliefs being transmitted from the minds of adults into the minds of children has always been happening in every culture around the world. This is no less true for indigenous cultures even though they may have no formal educational institutions. In those cultures, as children progress through childhood, they gradually spend more and more of each day watching, imitating, and learning from adults. Since our concept of "intellectual knowledge" may not even exist in the consciousness of indigenous cultures, there is probably no distinction between the teaching of beliefs and the teaching of methods and skills. Both are taught simultaneously. The process continues largely unabated through the innocence of childhood up through the onset of puberty, which generally triggers final training and initiation into adult status. At that point, there are almost always time-honored formal rituals and ceremonies to mark "graduation" into the surrounding culture's acceptance and recognition of full adult status. The process of instilling belief systems in the younger generation can be highly structured, formalized, and extensive as it is in modern western civilizations, or it can be totally organic as it is in cultures that are considered to be more primitive.

Even among those who continue to subordinate themselves well beyond the onset of adolescence, almost everyone reaches a point of making their own version of this declaration: "I'm in charge of the development and management of my life from now on." Regardless of when that declaration occurs, and regardless of whether it is met with frowns of disapproval or affirmations and celebrations from the surrounding culture, it marks the true beginning of "adult" consciousness. From this point on, most young adults in modern cultures go out into the world and try to live "the lives of their dreams" relying on whatever they have learned up to that time. Unfortunately, regardless of the chronological age at the time a person enters adult identity, unless they've done intentional work to purge themselves of dysfunctional beliefs, those beliefs will still be operating in their consciousness, affecting the content of what they perceive as well as the perspective from which they perceive it. Whatever they try to do, be, or become will almost inevitably be compromised by whatever dysfunctional beliefs they've absorbed along their paths to the present.

## The role of beliefs in frustration, irritation, and unhappiness

Few people are so completely happy they would say they are already living in their own personal versions of heaven. Most people have at least a few issues that continue to bother them on a long-term chronic basis. For some, it's a steady stream of minor irritations that pop up causing temporary mental and/or emotional dissonance, such as frustration, irritation, and/or unhappiness. Unfortunately, for some people, normal daily life is filled with these.

There's virtually no end to the number and variety of external causes people can identify as the sources of their dissonance: an unpleasant job, a failing relationship, the high cost of living, difficult co-workers, low pay, bureaucracy, corruption, the neighbor's dog, or simply a "bad hair day." Everyone has his or her own list of "causes" to blame for their unhappiness.

Most people try to improve their situations by using a variety of strategies to change or eliminate the external causes they've identified as the sources of their discomfort. Some use money and/or power in efforts to change or eliminate external causes. Others try to *acquire* more possessions, more money, more control, and more options with which they attempt to insulate themselves from the perceived causes. Still others concentrate on trying to *achieve* relief. They try to achieve a better outward appearance, more social status, more respect, more recognition, more pride, or more of whatever they believe will make them happier. But causes of discomfort are not static. They occur in an endlessly changing dynamic flow. No matter how much money or power you have, and no matter how much you change, eliminate, achieve, or acquire in battling that realm of external causes, you rarely "catch up" enough to rest. Even if you *do* manage to "catch up" occasionally, you don't *stay* "caught up" for long. ("It's just one damn thing after another.") Trying to change "external causes" of mental or emotional dissonance is like being caught on a hamster wheel. You run and you run, but even if you work *even harder* and run *even faster*, you rarely seem to *get there*.

Quite often, whatever you identify as "the cause" is considerably beyond your reach. You have little or *no* power to change it. You may not even have any opportunities to influence it. If trying to manipulate externals is your only strategy, then it's easy to understand why your reality probably feels like a harsh place. Here's the irony: what most people identify as "the cause" of their unhappiness or frustration is almost always perceived as something external – something "out there" in the world around them. But the real sources are almost never external. That "external cause" you try to blame is probably, at most, a trigger or catalyst. When you encounter it, you go into *feelings* of frustration, irritation, and/or unhappiness, but those feelings are actually a function of a *relationship* between one or more elements in your belief system and whatever you've mistakenly identified as "the cause" of your discomfort. It's a dysfunctional *relationship* that's the *real source* of your problem.

Fortunately, it's nearly always possible to change your internal end of any relationship in which you find yourself. Austrian psychiatrist Viktor Frankl wrote eloquently about this in his book, *Mans' Search for Meaning.* During World War II, Frankl was imprisoned in a Nazi concentration camp. While there, he observed that some prisoners endured and survived, while others seemed to "give up." Those who gave up were often the ones who died soonest. Frankl studied those who endured, and concluded that each one insisted on believing in a vision. Even in the midst of almost unimaginably harsh and cruel conditions, each survivor had a vision of surviving to live again in a much better future. From that observation, Frankl concluded that the crucial difference was attitude. While he acknowledged that his captors could take away almost everything that made him human, and they could make his circumstances almost unbearably harsh, the one thing they could *not* take away was his freedom to choose the *attitude* from which he regarded his situation. He realized that he could always control how he "played his hand." Frankl chose – in spite of extreme hardships and almost unimaginably difficult circumstances – to *believe in* his vision of a future in which he would survive. In that vision, Frankl imagined himself standing at the lectern in a well-appointed auditorium full of distinguished guests. He imagined giving a talk to fellow psychiatrists and neurologists about what he had experienced and observed, and how he and others had managed to survive the concentration camp. He developed a vision and made an intentional choice to believe in it. Frankl *did* survive to give those lectures, and he went on to write this wonderful book about his experiences.

Your belief system determines how you position yourself, i.e. how you "play your hand" in *every* relationship, and how you *experience* every relationship, regardless of whether you're relating to a person, a situation, or an entire culture.

Here's a much less dramatic example from my own experience. It's about a relationship between several elements in my belief system and the reality of Walmart. In the early 90's, I traveled by car across rural North Carolina on my way to vacation at the beach. In one small town after another, I saw a disturbing number of boarded up empty storefronts with "For Rent" signs. Almost without fail, at the edge of each town, there would be a big new Walmart. I concluded that Walmart had used its economic power to "play the bully" and had essentially "stolen" the economic lifeblood of the town. I also read numerous accounts describing Walmart's highly questionable — predatory and/or abusive? — personnel policies at that time. In my belief system, I started labeling Walmart as a "bad actor." I made Walmart my enemy. Beginning then and for years after, I refused to buy anything from Walmart. I would inconvenience myself, pay more, and sometimes go far out of my way to buy from any vendor *other* than Walmart. Through most of the'90's, just the sight of a Walmart store caused me to feel a little bit angry, a little bit sad, and quite often, depressed. However, the satisfaction of my personal boycott — refusing to shop there — gave me enough distance and insulation to provide an acceptable measure of relief from the dissonance caused by my dysfunctional beliefs about Walmart.

More than 20 years later in 2012, I found myself driving 18-wheelers all over the country, usually staying "out on the road" as much as three weeks at a time. (It was work I had done for a while in my '20's, and because I had really enjoyed then, I went back to it when I tired of professional bureaucracy.) When all the truck stop parking lots were full and I was still looking for a place to stop for the night, most Walmart stores welcomed me. Their stores usually gave me a safe, well-lit, fairly level place to park for the night, and their parking lots were usually big enough to allow relatively easy maneuvering in an 18-wheeler. Plus, their stores routinely stocked nearly everything a truck driver might need, from new socks, to flashlight batteries, to fresh fruit. With that change in employment, the satisfaction of my personal boycott became far more expensive. To accommodate, I changed my attitude.

I had learned in the ensuing years that part of the reason Walmart is so successful is that they use computer technology to constantly monitor sales trends. If sales of a particular item suddenly surge in Walmart stores in one area of the country, managers quickly check the demographics of that area, and then make sure that in every geographic area with similar demographics, that item is in good supply in all their stores in those areas. That struck me as an impressively creative way of using technology to drive exceptionally effective marketing. I also read that in spite of all the criticism, no other retailer does a better job of getting basic consumer needs and supplies onto their shelves and available to consumers at the lowest possible prices. We're not talking about extravagant luxuries here. We're talking about laundry detergent, peanut butter, toilet tissue, and all the other basic needs and supplies nearly all consumers *must buy* on a regular basis. I began to recognize that, in spite of my earlier reasons for boycotting, Walmart performs a valuable service for millions who live in financially challenging circumstances.

In the years between my travels in coastal North Carolina in the '90's and my time driving 18-wheelers more than 20 years later, very little of the reality of Walmart in my world had changed. However, my *experience* of being in relationship with Walmart *did* change: I made an adjustment in my belief system by changing an attitude. I chose to stop judging Walmart as an evil oppressor, even though most of the factors that once led me to that attitude and perspective were – and continue to be – very real. Instead of prioritizing my perspective on Walmart as a Bad Actor, I switched my priority to perceiving Walmart as an important resource for me as a driver of 18-wheelers, and for millions of others who can't really afford to shop anywhere else. Both perspectives have ample justification, and both are valid. Each can lead to its own reality. But the choice between the two perspectives is purely arbitrary. I changed my attitude and perspective about Walmart. I made adjustments in my belief system, and that made a world of positive difference in my life as a truck driver.

In much the same way, the elements in your belief system largely determine how you perceive and experience your reality. If you're feeling irritated or frustrated, it's easy, tempting, and basic human nature to identify an "external cause" and blame that. However, it's more productive to remember that your discomfort is usually a function of the *relationship* between one or more elements of your belief system and that "external cause" you've identified. Changing those relationships – by adjusting your beliefs – is usually the most efficient and effective way to remove the discomfort and restore happiness. Remember Victor Frankl's observation: you *always* have the power to change your experience of *any* relationship you're in simply by adjusting your beliefs – by changing how you "play your hand."

## Living with dysfunctional beliefs

Assuming you have at least one or more dysfunctional beliefs, still operating (and keeping you grounded when you want so much to be soaring,) you've probably been accommodating those dysfunctional beliefs in one of three ways:

1. Trying to change or eliminate the external cause
2. Trying to ignore the internal dissonance, i.e., the unhappiness, frustration, irritation, etc.
3. Trying to mitigate the dissonance by insulating or anesthetizing yourself

Trying to change or eliminate an external causes can require a lot of resources. Consider the time and effort required to bring about social or political change on any level. Using the legal system to change or eliminate an external source of dissonance can be similarly expensive and time consuming. Furthermore, success is not guaranteed in any of these arenas, no matter how much time, effort, and money you spend. If you're trying to change or eliminate an even more local and particular focus of dissonance by exercising personal choices, there's still no guarantee you'll be successful, and even this strategy can consume significant resources. Consider this example: if you have a dysfunctional belief regarding authority, you're unlikely to find a more satisfying work situation simply by changing jobs. Even the most wonderful "new boss" will trigger the dysfunctional relationship the first time he or she exercises authority in a manner that triggers your dysfunctional beliefs about authority. It's almost inevitable that you'll find yourself caught in the same uncomfortable dynamic that caused you to leave the old job. (Note also that changing jobs is usually expensive in multiple ways. It can cause tremendous upheaval, requiring significant expenditures of time, energy, attention, and sometimes money.)

In the earlier example of my relationship with Walmart, I was living in a negative and judgmental attitude toward something that I encountered frequently in my reality. That belief was causing a measure of internal dissonance. Option #1 was never even feasible. I had no power to affect Walmart's corporate decisions about where to build new stores, and I was similarly powerless regarding their personnel policies. Option #2 wasn't realistic, either. I couldn't simply ignore the "external cause" of my dissonance, because there are Walmart stores just about everywhere in the United States. And I wasn't willing to move to a foreign country to resolve my discomfort. Until I started driving 18-wheelers, Option #3 was working well enough for me. I was enduring the discomfort caused by my attitude, and offsetting that discomfort with the satisfaction of boycotting Walmart most of the time. When I started the new job, my situation changed dramatically. Option #3 was no longer acceptable, because the satisfaction of boycotting was no longer strong enough to offset the inconvenience my boycott was causing.

My original reasons for choosing to perceive and relate to Walmart as a "bad actor" were still legitimate, but choosing to see Walmart as a vendor providing a valuable service for lots of people (including myself!) was equally legitimate. The choice was arbitrary, and it was clear that I would suffer no significant negative consequences from either choice. It made good sense to intentionally change my attitude. I made the adjustment, and enjoyed the benefits that Walmart offered for the rest of the time I drove 18-wheelers. I left truck driving 2014, but I've kept the changed attitude. My adjusted attitude was and continues to be a better choice for me.

## The possibility of changing your beliefs

You may be surprised to realize that *most* of the attitudes, assumptions, perspectives, etc. in your belief system are completely arbitrary. There is no external authority requiring that any specific beliefs *must* be —or must *not* be — included in anyone's belief system. Rules and laws prescribe and prohibit *behaviors*, but they rarely attempt to specify what must be or must not be part of your belief system. Therefore, *you are surprisingly free to make adjustments* in your beliefs. So long as you're careful to avoid triggering unmanageable consequences, you have an enormous amount of freedom to fine-tune your beliefs intentionally and strategically. In fact, through careful fine-tuning of your belief system, you can radically re-shape your experience of reality.

It is entirely possible to intentionally choose beliefs that are different from – even diametrically opposed to -- the beliefs you learned early, which have always – so far – served as the foundation of your consciousness. Perhaps the most dramatic example is when a person has a "born again" religious conversion. In this kind of change, the person gives up his or her own sense of authority over a whole range of beliefs, and yields that authority to the guidance and/or teachings of a charismatic teacher, religion, or a religious institution.

These "conversions" are remarkable for how quickly they can shift a person's entire way of being in the world, and bring dramatic change to their overall experience of living. Unfortunately, such radical shifts in belief systems are often triggered when a person is facing a major loss, failure, or catastrophe, with no apparent survival path available. The person experiences a psychological dynamic I call "impending psychic annihilation." For most people, it takes this extreme level of intense motivation to make the kind of sudden radical changes in beliefs that are typical in a religious conversion. Another common example occurs when a long-term alcoholic or addict successfully "kicks the habit." In each of these situations, the person has made a conscious decision to change his or her belief system in response to overwhelming "causes," and the results are often as dramatic as night and day.

More often, people make changes in their belief systems more gradually and in smaller increments. It's what you do when you learn effectively from "the school of hard knocks." Our focus here, in learning to soar, is learning to make adjustments that are somewhere between the extremes described above. Until you're a lot more familiar with your belief system and how to manage it, trying for a "radical conversion" is probably not going to be successful. However, it's not necessary to wait around for the next "hard knock" to happen, either. You can start working on more modest adjustments immediately.

Almost everyone makes subtle adjustments in their belief systems as they go through the normal experiences of growing up and living into adult life. Some reach a stopping point, at which they decide, "OK, I guess this is how life is. I'll just have to make the best of it from here on." Others continue to seek a more satisfying and fulfilling experience of living. They continue paying attention and learning from their experiences. Those who learn to soar are the ones who live most intentionally and intensely. And quite often, these are the people who continue making incremental adjustments and refinements in their beliefs throughout their years as adults, and even into old age. This lifelong practice enables them to soar ever higher.

# Two examples of common beliefs you can change

You are free to adjust your beliefs to support whatever reality you desire most. For our first example, let's look at guilt, a particularly common dysfunctional belief. Quite often it's a generalized feeling of guilt that is not directly associated with any particular words you've said or actions you've taken. You weren't born with this kind of unfocused guilt. You were *taught* how to experience it, perhaps *encouraged* to feel it, maybe even *rewarded* for making a habit of feeling it. When the authority figures in your young life said things like, "You should be ashamed of yourself," they were teaching you and encouraging you to feel this kind of guilt. Now that you're an adult, notice that continuing to feel this kind of guilt is mostly a bad habit. Unless you're in an extremely dysfunctional relationship, feeling generalized unfocused guilt doesn't win you any kind of positive points on any scorecard anywhere. It has no redeeming value whatsoever.

If you decide this kind of guilt is no longer serving you in any acceptable way, you can give it up. Simply stop believing in guilt, stop acting as if it's necessary or helpful, and leave it behind. You can still take full responsibility for specific words you said or actions you took, and for any pain, damage, or destruction you may have inadvertently caused in the past or may cause in the future. You can apologize sincerely and offer to make reparations. Meanwhile, you are totally free to stop choosing unfocused generalized guilt. (With guilt, the tricky thing is to avoid feeling guilty about having given it up!) You just have to find the courage to drag your unfocused guilt out in the open, hold it up to the light, and evaluate: Is this belief serving me well? Do I *really* want this affecting everything I am and everything I try to do in the future? If your answer is "no", you have the option of leaving it behind by replacing it with a belief that will serve you better. For example, assert the belief that you are completely OK just the way you are, and remind yourself there is absolutely nothing in the natural environment demanding or requiring that you feel unfocused generalized guilt. After you make that assertion, practice believing and feeling a new reality in which you are completely OK and acceptable *without the usual guilt.* Practice with fierce determination. It may feel foreign and awkward at first, but practice makes perfect.

For a second example, let's look at another common dysfunctional belief, "I'm not good enough." If you received too many critical and harshly judgmental messages as a child, you may well have incorporated this dysfunctional belief deep into your own self-image. Critical peer pressure during adolescence may have made it worse. Today, this belief may have become so powerful and so deep that you hardly even notice how often it limits your sense of what you are worthy to receive and experience, and what you are capable of learning, doing, and becoming. Lots of people suffer from some version of this. It can be so severe that it's almost debilitating. For others, it's less severe and is experienced more as a nuisance. For you, it may be nearly impossible to even imagine a version of yourself that does not include its limitations. Nevertheless, you *can* intentionally choose to replace this dysfunctional belief with its opposite: "I *am* good enough to receive, experience, learn, do, and become whatever my heart desires." You *can* succeed in this. The process requires commitment, perseverance, and practice, but it *is* possible.

There's no shortage of training programs and self-help advice advocating the power of positive affirmations, so this notion will probably seem familiar. However, for these "self-help affirmations" to be effective, you have to take the long view. If you've always felt "not good enough," simply repeating an affirmation – some version of "I *am* good enough," – may feel totally unnatural or even uncomfortable, especially when you first begin. It may feel as if you're saying someone *else's* words that have nothing to do with you. It might even feel ridiculous to continue. You may feel silly for daring to believe that countless repetitions of such an assertion could possibly be helpful. For all of these reasons, even if you decide to go through the motions of practicing, you will probably be tempted to give up and abandon the effort long before you make enough progress to become aware of any positive change.

However, if you commit to the process by daring to *really* believe – in a deep and powerful way – that it *is* possible to replace an old belief that you're "not good enough," you'll be creating new space in your consciousness from which a new belief can start to play a powerful role in your vision of your future. Then, with persistent practice, a much more positive belief about your worthiness can begin to seem like a normal and comfortable part of who you are and how you know yourself. The success of Alcoholics Anonymous is undeniable, and they have an almost identical technique in their methods: They refer to it as, "Fake it 'til you make it." No matter how unreal it may seem at first, if you dare to practice a reality you would like to move into, and if you really work at *believing* it and *feeling* — with as much intensity as you can — whenever you practice, you'll gradually become more successful at *actually* believing it and feeling it sometimes. When you've practiced so much that it becomes easy to believe it and feel it most of the time – without even having to think about it – you'll realize that you've *already* moved into the new reality you were intending to create for yourself.

## Learning to recognize dysfunctional beliefs

Whatever you're doing, whatever you're thinking about, whatever you're experiencing, if you don't already feel like you're soaring, there's probably a dysfunctional belief that's causing you to feel heavy and grounded. Next time you find yourself feeling irritated or unhappy with something that seems to be "outside" in the environment around you, take a moment to go through your beliefs, one by one, asking yourself, "Which of my beliefs are operating in my experience of this situation?" Simply go through each of the nine categories – attitudes, assumptions, beliefs, perspectives, values, expectations, hopes, fears, and attachments – and for each one, look carefully to see if and how there might be a belief that's contributing to the dissonance you're experiencing. *(You can review definitions for each of the nine categories of beliefs on page 53.)* Start with attitudes. Ask yourself, "Which of my attitudes are operating in this unpleasant experience?" If you don't find any attitudes, then move on to assumptions, and then beliefs, perspectives, values, and so on. If you're willing to be completely honest, you'll almost always find at least one or more dysfunctional beliefs, i.e., beliefs that are simply not consistent with the fundamental realities of human living in time and space, that are playing an active role in your unhappiness or discomfort.

Unless you have already looked carefully at your discomfort or unhappiness in detail, you may not initially be able to recognize the dysfunctional belief that's causing your dissonance. You may need to start by focusing on a specific part of a situation in which you're unhappy. Let whatever unhappiness you've selected flow into your immediate experience. Dare to allow it to fill your immediate experience completely. Then try to become clear and accurate about every detail of it. (If there's emotional pain involved, remember that pain itself doesn't damage you; efforts to *deny* or *escape* from pain are more likely to cause damage than pain itself.) You'll probably find that your unhappiness or discomfort is much more complex than you initially thought. In fact, when you start looking closely, you're more likely to find a thick rope than a single fiber. What seems simple enough on the surface when you complain about it to a friend is often an entire constellation of contributing irritations, and each of *those* may include several contributing components. Analyze your unhappiness until you get to know *all* the parts of it. Keep breaking it down into component discomforts and irritations until you arrive at elements that can't be broken down any further.

# An example: Getting to know my anger in detail

My best example of "getting to know a discomfort or unhappiness in detail" would be from my own experience with personal anger. It's been a long process with many iterations, because anger is a complex form of discomfort and unhappiness. (My work on this continues to be an evolving process, and it may never be fully "completed.") I had to get to know my anger well enough to be able to identify its various components. For each component, I had to identify the dysfunctional belief that was causing the problem, and for some components, more than one belief was involved.

Before launching into the full explanation of how I'e made significant progress in learning to manage my anger, it might be helpful to know about a major gap in my early education. When I entered my adult years, the only technique I had learned for dealing with anger was suppressing it. Consequently, I had a huge backlog of suppressed anger. Sometimes, new and even relatively minor irritations would cause my "storage capacity" to overflow. In my late 20's and 30's, certain kinds of interactions and situations could trigger an almost immediate anger in which my stomach muscles would tighten, my breathing would become rapid and shallow, and my voice would shake if I tried to speak. Fortunately, my values around respect were strong enough that I have never attacked anyone physically, and only rarely have I "attacked" anyone verbally. However, I can be surprisingly articulate when I'm angry, and I've made some seriously harsh and hard-hitting statements in anger.

Here's the story of how I (mostly) learned to recognize the beliefs that were contributing to my anger: I started looking for patterns and common elements in the situations in which I became angry. The first insight was that it was almost always *interpersonal expectations* that triggered my anger. For example, if I made arrangements to attend a concert, planned my time around it, and was looking forward to it, learning that the concert had been cancelled might trigger intense disappointment, but since it was not an *interpersonal* disappointment, it probably would not trigger my anger. However, if a close friend had agreed to go with me, and that friend called to cancel at the last minute, or worse, failed to show up, I might feel significant anger.

The next insight was realizing that the intensity and importance of the interpersonal dynamic had a big influence, also. *Strangers* passing through my world had relatively little power to trigger my anger. I might be totally disgusted with their actions, or the values revealed by their actions, but unless they interacted with me in a direct, one-on-one manner, they rarely triggered any anger. That narrowed the focus down to people I interacted with more personally. I was able to identify four separate categories of those interactions, any one of which could trigger my anger:

1. *Not being heard* – I quickly became angry if the person I was talking with didn't take the time – or was unwilling to make the effort – to listen carefully to what I was saying and assess its value before continuing on with what they were saying.

   Here's a little personal history to help explain why "feeling heard" was so important to me: As I was growing up, doing well in school was the one behavior that earned me the "warm fuzzies" of acceptance and affirmation that I so craved from my parents. Doing well in school brought me more and richer doses of emotional support than any other behavior, so doing well in school – i.e., being smart enough to have the right answer, and even better, being the *first* to come up with the right answer – became a primary strategy for obtaining emotional support. As a young adult, if I found myself in a conversation about something I cared about with someone I knew and respected, I would do my best to make constructive contributions to the dialogue. In those situations, if the other person seemed unwilling to spend the time or make the effort to really understand the content I was offering, I would usually feel unappreciated, disrespected, and cut off from the emotional support I needed. On an emotional level, I became angry because I felt threatened, similar to the way a wild animal can become angry and aggressive if it feels threatened.

There were actually three variations of "not being heard:"

a. *The other person proved incapable of understanding* – If I could see that the other person was sincerely trying to understand, but not able to grasp my point, I might become a little bit angry. (My anger in such situations was frequently amplified if I held an *expectation* or made an *assumption* that the person I was talking with *should* be capable of understanding.)

b. *The other person obviously understood, but intentionally ignored my point* -- In my belief system, if I'm in a disagreement with someone, and that person makes a statement that clearly and obviously has validity and relevance, I may wish the person hadn't said it, wish it weren't true, and/or wish I didn't have to deal with it. But *ignoring* the statement – in hopes that ignoring it will somehow make it go away – seems fundamentally disrespectful and intellectually bankrupt to me. My values around intellectual integrity require me to at least acknowledge such a statement for its validity, no matter how inconvenient or uncomfortable it is. Finding myself in a conversation in which someone seemed to be intentionally denying the validity of what I was trying to contribute would trigger my anger. Encountering that behavior conflicted with my assumptions and expectations that everyone should value intellectual integrity as highly as I do.

c.  *The other person was so intent on "winning" that they attempted to refute my contribution by attacking it from every possible angle, even from perspectives that had no relevance whatsoever to the subject we were discussing.* Exaggeration and sarcasm are especially toxic versions of this. Emotionally, I experienced these responses as aggressive bullying, which triggered my values around fairness, respect, and honesty. (I can respect winning, but only if you win fairly.)

2.  *Failure to honor agreements* was a second hair trigger. I once got into a huge conflict with a co-worker because she intentionally chose not to honor a professional agreement we had made. We were scheduled to meet with a client, and we had discussed in advance exactly what we would be trying to accomplish in the meeting and what our strategy would be. When the meeting unfolded, the client presented new information we had not anticipated. Without any consultation with me, my co-worker completely abandoned both the strategy we had agreed to use and the final result we had agreed to seek. Suddenly, in the middle of the meeting, she was taking the client's perspective, advocating for his position, and opposing me. I became livid! This was a violation of my expectations about how we would work together in the meeting, and on a deeper level, it was a violation of my assumptions regarding her capacity for and commitment to professionalism.

3. *Limited capacity for considering new possibilities* was – and still is -- another personal characteristic that can trigger my anger. My mind naturally tends toward creative possibilities for making things better. Accepting and respecting current realities, when they seem unnecessarily limiting, is difficult for me. When I find myself dealing with bureaucracies in which processes seem to me to be far more complicated and inefficient than necessary, I'm often inclined to see and offer suggestions for improvements. When a person in a responsible administrative position demonstrates little or no capacity for considering a new idea about a better way of doing things, and instead, offers nothing other than blind allegiance and defense of a status quo that is not serving me well, I tend to lose patience quickly and become quite angry. I realize now that it's unrealistic of me to expect others to be as capable as I feel in imagining and considering new ideas and the possible advantages of changes to the status quo.

4. *Intentional dishonesty* — I'm not willing to adjust how much I value honesty in others and myself. However, I have learned that holding honesty as a value causes me to become angry less often if I modify my *expectation* that everyone I encounter should value honesty as highly as I do. When I was younger and much more naïve, I assumed everyone was honest. That led to some painful surprises. I have learned that my assumptions about honesty need constant monitoring and adjustment, based on a careful assessment of what I know about the particular person with whom I'm interacting. I have learned that it's usually OK for me to *assume* that people I know well and choose to respect will be honest with me. I

value honesty as highly as ever, but I no longer extend that assumption of honesty to everyone.

The most recent insight on managing my anger is that the intensity of my anger is a function of how much I value my relationship with the person toward whom I feel angry. If I'm in a disagreement with someone and my relationship with that person is *very* important to me on a deeply personal level – a long-time friend or a lover, for example – that person's capacity to trigger my anger is stronger, and I need to be especially careful. With a supervisor or co-worker, not so much. With a bureaucratic administrator whom I may only encounter occasionally, there's much less capacity. With a total stranger, the capacity for triggering my anger is relatively low.

I know now that if I begin to feel conflict with someone, or if I'm going into an interaction in which I want to convince or persuade someone, I need to prepare by assessing the importance of the relationship. How much do I *value* it? The more I value it, the more carefully I need to monitor my emotional responses, so that I can take corrective action if anger starts to develop.

The bottom line to these examples is that I have repeatedly experienced discomfort (anger) in response to the actions and choices of others. Before I started learning to fine-tune my belief system, I blamed what I perceived to be the external cause, i.e., the person or situation that was the target of my anger. Over the years, as I've learned to understand my angry tendencies in much more detail, I've been able to identify a variety of beliefs, values, assumptions, and expectations that have all contributed to my many experiences of anger. By making adjustments in my belief system and how I manage it, I've been able to greatly reduce both the frequency and intensity of anger in my life.

# The first decision in managing beliefs

Let's assume that you've discovered a belief that is probably a factor in your discomfort. At this point, the important question to ask yourself is, "Am I *willing* to modify this belief?" Some elements of your belief system are probably sacred. You may be fundamentally opposed to adjusting any of those. For example, I value honesty and integrity. I'm not willing to set those values aside for any reason. If the belief you've identified is non-negotiable, you can choose one of the three options below, or some combination of these options:

1.  Continue the belief while trying to eliminate the external cause of your discomfort. (As stated earlier, this strategy can consume huge resources, and rarely brings sustained relief.)

2.  Continue the belief with a commitment to ignore the discomfort.

3.  Continue the belief, with a commitment to endure the discomfort by putting as much insulating distance as possible between yourself and the "external cause."

In my Walmart example above, Options #1 and #2 were both out of the question. Although Option#3 had been working satisfactorily for almost 20 years, a change in my job circumstances rendered that strategy unacceptable. Fortunately, there's nearly always Option #4: Make an adjustment in your beliefs.

To summarize, adjusting a belief is usually quicker and easier than trying to change an "external "cause." Adjusting one or more beliefs may also be an easier and more satisfying choice than enduring the costs, or putting extra distance between yourself and the "external cause." The final benefit is that adjusting a belief is the usually the most effective strategy for both bringing relief for the immediate discomfort *and* for reducing the likelihood that you'll be "hooked" by any similar "external cause" in the future.

# How to change a belief

When you first identify a dysfunctional belief, and you begin to recognize all the ways it has not been serving you well – all the ways it has cost you and limited you in the past – you may feel some despair. You may be tempted to criticize yourself harshly and beat yourself up emotionally. If you experience that temptation, follow these steps instead:

1. **Remember that the belief you want to change only exists in your mind.** It has no external corollary in the physical world. No matter how many other people share this belief, and no matter how strongly they believe it and live by it, *you* are the one who has created *all the reality* and *all the power* this belief has ever had in *your* life. Give yourself a congratulatory "pat on the back" for being so powerfully creative, (even though the content of your creation is not what you want anymore!

2. **Realize that you can now use the *exact same* creative power you've been using to sustain this dysfunctional belief — probably since childhood when you created it — to replace it** with a different belief that will serve you better.

3. **Choose a *new* belief** that promises to serve you better

4. **Start practicing.** Pretend the *new* belief is already part of you. Practice *feeling* the new belief with such intensity that you become *highly effective* at pretending it, i.e., making it seem real. (As stated earlier, Alcoholics Anonymous refers

to this strategy as, "Fake it 'til you make it." It's actively and widely taught in AA, *because it works!*)

5.  **Continue practicing** until you find yourself "pretending" the new belief without even thinking about what you're doing. (When you arrive there, you'll already be *living* in your new reality.)

This is true with *any* belief you may want to replace. Some examples would be a belief that you chose the wrong profession or the wrong partner, or that you hate holidays or moving or changing jobs, or an idea that you're not worthy to have and do and be all that you dream of. *Any* belief that causes you to feel or act as if the ideal reality you long for is not fully accessible can simply be left behind by actively replacing it with a different belief that will serve you better. Even though the dysfunctional belief may be a comfortably familiar part of how you have always thought of yourself, leaving it behind by replacing it with a more satisfying belief will not cause anything bad to happen. Moreover, you'll *feel* a whole lot better and you'll probably become more effective at moving toward the life you want most. (In fact, some would say that when you leave a dysfunctional belief behind, the Universe celebrates!)

It's important to begin with this important perspective: you're attempting to change a reality that you have spent years creating. That's the same as years of *practicing* a reality, as if it were part of a role you've been playing in a theatrical production. Practice makes perfect. If you've spent years practicing a belief that you're not good enough, you've probably become highly effective at making that belief your reality. Every time this dysfunctional belief has been activated in your consciousness, you have actually been *practicing* and *perfecting your ability* to create a version of your reality in which you really *aren't* good enough. The natural result of all that practice is that you're now *an expert* at feeling and therefore, *being* "not good enough." You've wandered into a habit of creating a reality you no longer want, and now you feel stuck in it. (Don't worry. You're not alone, and there *is* a way out.)

Before you even start trying to change a belief, it's important to recognize that when attempting this kind of work on yourself, your orientation is extremely important. If you think of what you're trying to do as "moving away" from a belief, or "leaving a belief behind," you'll find that progress is difficult and ultimately impossible. You can only move *toward* a new vision of a different reality in which the old belief (which you no longer want,) has no more reality. In your new vision, the new belief (which you're intentionally choosing) is already firmly established *now*, in the present (and not in some distant "future,") as an active element in your belief system. The belief you're leaving behind must become so irrelevant that it's not even worth the effort required to remember it. To shut down its reality and its power, make sure you spend *all* of your attention and all of your effort on practicing the new and more desirable belief instead.

Consider this analogy. If you're in a boat on the open sea, and you're trying to steer your vessel away from a buoy – to "get away from it" or "leave it behind" – the reference point by which you're steering is the very thing you want to be done with. If you succeed in going far enough to *nearly* lose sight of it, a part of you will realize that further "success" in moving away from it will mean you'll no longer have any reference point to steer by and no destination to steer toward. At the moment you can no longer see the buoy you've been trying to get away from, your status will suddenly shift to "lost." The uncertainty – even fear – you might feel in anticipation of "being lost" may cause you to slow your progress, turn back, or go into a circling pattern *around* the buoy, just so you can keep your reference point in view. Trying to move *away from* anything is almost always futile.

It's far more effective to steer *toward* a different buoy, a different island, and preferably, a vision of yourself living in a different and much more desirable reality as you move into the future. You may not be able to see it very clearly – maybe even not at all – from where you're beginning. (Not yet, anyway.) However, your vision of the reality you want to live into is your compass. When you're moving *toward* your vision, whatever you're leaving behind becomes irrelevant from the very first moment you begin. If you're in the most helpful orientation, the moment when that old belief slips out of sight behind you is hardly even noticeable and not worth mentioning. When that moment happens, you won't suddenly feel lost. Instead, you'll feel that moment – if you notice it at all – as a milestone of progress, enabling you to continue toward your vision with re-invigorated enthusiasm. You'll also experience a surge of confidence in that moment, because you'll have dramatic proof that you're making progress, even though you may not be able to see your ultimate destination yet.

# What to expect when you try to change a belief

If you decide to start making changes in your beliefs, you need to be aware of several arenas in which you may encounter resistance. The first is the physical arena of time and space. This one is the least tolerant. Believing you can fly does not enable you to jump off a cliff and survive. Believing you can breathe under water will likely cause you to drown. Believing that you can deny the laws of physics in time and space will almost always bring unpleasant natural consequences.

So long as you keep your new beliefs private, the social environment around you is more accepting. It has no firm requirements about what is *in* – or *not in* – your belief system. In most cases, there won't be any *naturally occurring* consequences for making adjustments in your beliefs. You can choose to believe there is no "god," and you'll find that the world around you is abundant with intellectually credible evidence that there really is no "god." Or, you can believe that there *is* a "god," and the world you'll experience will give you all kinds of evidence that God is real. (As stated earlier, beliefs determine what you perceive, how you perceive it, and ultimately, how you experience reality.) You can also choose to believe that it's better not to make a definitive choice either way on the "god" question. In that case, you'll find yourself "living on the fence," year after year, because sometimes you'll see compelling evidence *for*, and other times you'll see compelling evidence *against* the reality of any kind of "god." Believing in a god can lead to a perfectly acceptable reality. Not believing in a god also seems to work well enough for lots of people. And if you find yourself permanently "stuck in the middle" no one is going to be upset or experience any discomfort from your ambivalence (except *you*, perhaps.) Whatever you decide to believe about the possible existence of a god, your social environment may not even react in any noticeable way.

Here's another example: You can choose to believe that it's vitally important to be at least middle class. If you do, you'll probably find yourself judging others whom you perceive to be at a lower socio-economic level than your own, and envying others whom you perceive to be at a higher level. On the other hand, you can choose to believe that the importance of socio-economic status is highly over-rated. If you make that choice, you will probably find yourself becoming acquainted and making friends and feeling comfortable with people all up and down the socio-economic spectrum. Either way, your social environment may not even notice. As stated earlier, you are free to change almost any of your beliefs at any time. However, the particular collection of beliefs you choose to keep will greatly determine the qualities and feelings of the reality in which you'll find yourself living.

The social environment will be relatively tolerant of changes so long as you refrain from advertising or promoting beliefs that are dramatically different from – or contrary to – the prevailing social norms. However, if you choose to be overt about choosing different beliefs, and if those beliefs are outside the prevailing norms, the social environment may impose subtle but powerful consequences. Peer pressure can be so light and subtle that it's almost playful. It can also be so deadly serious and overt that it tears families, friendships, and communities apart. There's no rule or law that says you are *required* to seek and win acceptance, respect, or approval from other people. But if you exhibit words and actions that signal you are operating from a dramatically different belief system, and if the people around you perceive that your belief system is directly contradictory or even *threatening* to their belief system, they'll probably be fearful. For members of a tightly involved group of people who cling together for comfort and safety, it's frightening to encounter someone who apparently has no need to enjoy their approval and no desire to share their beliefs or be part of their group. Frightened people sometimes lash out with aggressive and irrational behaviors. Nevertheless, you are actually free to choose whether to let others' responses bother you enough to affect your choices.

The institutional environment is entirely different. This is the realm of formally adopted rules and laws. Some institutions are big enough and powerful enough to have their own enforcement agencies. The University of Chicago, for example, has the world's largest private police department. Every government has some sort of official law (rule) enforcement agency. Governments don't just stop at enforcement; they also punish. They have systems of courts, which can impose fines and/or lock you up for days, months, sometimes years. Some even impose the ultimate punishment – death by execution – for breaking their rules. If your beliefs lead to external words or actions that signal to the surrounding institutional system that you are not in compliance with their rules and laws, official "gate keepers" of those systems will probably enforce consequences. They want everyone to stay within the defined and officially sanctioned parameters and remain compliant. The police may arrest you and the courts may put you on trial and fine you and/or lock you up. A university may expel you, an employer may fire you, a professional association may revoke your license to practice their profession, the American Kennel Club may bar you from showing your dog for the next two years, or you can be kicked out of the bowling league. All of these are examples of the kinds of consequences you can bring down on yourself if you're not careful about how much you reveal about any unusual adjustments you make that might put you outside the prevailing belief system's norms.

Here's a key for managing your beliefs in the context your environment: Live internally by whatever beliefs you choose, but take care to show respect and tolerance for those who fully subscribe to the prevailing beliefs around you. To avoid triggering unwanted consequences, choose your external words and actions to be sure they demonstrate the required minimum levels of responsibility and respect for the relevant physical, social, political, economic, and institutional systems. So long as you "pay those dues," you are mostly free to modify your beliefs any way you want. In fact, you are free to live in a very different reality. If you look around, you'll see people actually doing this. They are the artists and poets, the eccentrics, radicals, mavericks and weirdos. Look closely. No matter how unusual – noticeably outside the usual norms – they become, so long as they meet the prescribed minimums of responsibility and show appropriate respect to all aspects of their surrounding situations, they are usually allowed to continue in their eccentric lives.

# What if your efforts fail to produce the better experience you seek?

Occasionally, you might think you've identified a dysfunctional belief, but when you try to adjust it, nothing happens. You don't experience any relief. Sometimes the actual dysfunctional belief that's getting in your way has been a part of you for so long that it has become deeply integrated into your normal background, almost as if it has "gone into hiding." Try this 3-step process if you feel like your efforts to adjust a belief are not yielding the results you seek:

1. Consider the possibility that you've been aiming your efforts at the wrong target.
2. Think carefully – again – about the part of your reality you want to experience differently.
3. Ask yourself: "What *other* belief might someone hold that could lead to this same unpleasant reality?" Start making a list. You may come up with a dozen or more such beliefs. It

may take a while, but you will probably discover a different belief that's *actually* at the root of your internal dissonance. When that happens, you'll feel a distinctive mental "lurch.' (Don't worry, it will be unmistakable.) That's how you'll know you've found the dysfunctional belief that's *actually* responsible for your unhappiness or discomfort. Efforts to adjust this belief will almost certainly be more productive.

A different strategy you may need to consider is making an inventory of all that you feel fearful and/or guilty about. Guilt and fear separate you from yourself. They make it difficult to be clear about how your own reality is operating. Start by making a list. Consider each of the guilt and fear items you've listed, one at a time. For each one, ask yourself, "Is there any way this guilt (or fear) could be distorting my clarity about the belief(s) responsible for my discomfort? The participation of a trusted friend who knows you well can be helpful in this process.

## Four important considerations as you start adjusting your beliefs

**1. Start slowly --** The fact that you have the *capacity* to modify your belief system should not be taken as a license to go "hog wild" and start trying to run your life from a completely self-centered and self-indulgent belief system. Shared belief systems are the foundations of unity and coherence in a culture. Without shared beliefs, the communication needed for cooperation becomes much more difficult. The sense of community that can give you a warm feeling of belonging becomes nearly impossible without shared belief systems.

Today, the internet – especially Facebook – enables people to find, connect with, and retreat into tiny obscure pockets of reality. Some of these pockets can be extremely supportive and healthy for the people who spend time there. But some people retreat into other pockets and spend most – if not all—of their human interaction time, expressing and mutually reinforcing beliefs that have become unhinged from society's common core in ways that are not helpful to anyone. In chat groups and on blogs, those who have disconnected in unhealthy ways can mutually reinforce their commitments to dysfunctional beliefs until they become radicalized into splinter groups, no longer capable of making any positive contributions, no longer capable of reasonable constructive dialogue, and increasingly disruptive to society as a whole. Terrorism is the extreme expression of this. Radically disconnecting from the core beliefs of your surrounding situation can bring serious difficulties. Be careful.

**2. Take advantage of available guidance systems** -- If you're planning to attempt any serious disconnecting from one or more of the core beliefs of the society around you, it's best to use some sort of guidance system. Again, there are lot of institutions offering all sorts of resources to help you choose beliefs that have consistently helped others find liberating, empowering, and fulfilling experiences of reality. Almost any librarian would also be happy to help you locate such resources.

**Words of caution about religious and spiritual guidance on beliefs**

There are no requirements and no restrictions on the contents of your belief system. You can adopt any beliefs you can imagine, and you can do your best to live into the resulting realities. However, without careful choices, the new beliefs you choose may produce an experience of hell, rather than an experience of any heaven you would choose intentionally. Historically, four major belief systems – Christianity, with 31.5% of the world's population; Islam with 23.2%; Hinduism with 15.0%; and Buddhism with 7.1% – have been in the business of advocating beliefs and belief systems they claim will lead to more satisfying experiences of reality. The youngest of these systems has been around for centuries; the oldest for millennia. For each of these four main systems, the beliefs have endured, because they have stood the test of time. People who have been adopting them and living from within them have consistently given positive and enthusiastic reports on their experiences. (Note: This is a good example of healthy empirical investigating and knowing.)

You can take all the time you want or need to find replacement beliefs that can help stabilize, empower, and liberate your life. You can "try out" any new belief you want, and you can "test drive" it for as long as you need before making a decision to permanently adopt it or continue searching. However, hit-or-miss searching can consume months, if not years, of your life, and during that time, you're likely to continue having less than satisfying experiences. You may want to consider religious and spiritual teachings as a more direct path to the beliefs that will enable you to live the life you seek.

Unfortunately, religious organizations are enigmatic, and require careful consideration. First, it's important to recognize that while religious organizations may vigorously promote and advocate religious and spiritual "truths," those activities do not make them any more pure, holy, or sacred than any other organization. Religion and spirituality may be the *content* they are about, but that's not the same as *who they are*. Their focus on religious and spiritual *content* does nothing to change the fact that they are, nevertheless, *secular* organizations. They are organized, operated, and perpetuated by normal humans, so they are afflicted and limited by all the same internal organizational politics and occasional "bad actors" as giant for-profit corporations, governmental bureaucracies, and every other kind of secular organization.

To maintain their continuity as viable organizations, some religious organizations embellish stories, twist interpretations, and burden their teachings with staggering amounts of elaborate ritual and restrictive dogma. Such politically motivated modifications may temporarily help religious organizations grow in membership and become politically and/or financially "stronger." However, such changes typically dilute the strength of the original realities and beliefs that spawned them. When this happens, the new beliefs they championed, which originally seemed fresh, robust, and liberating, become so obscured by modifications and overlays of ritual and dogma, that their transformative power becomes largely inaccessible. To anyone trying to replace dysfunctional beliefs with more effective ones, the teachings offered by mainstream religious organizations can seem obscure, stale, anemic, and enslaving. It's little wonder many organized religions around the world are in decline.

When turning to these sources for guidance on beliefs, it can be extremely difficult to "separate the wheat from the chaff." On the other hand, it's important to remember that these organizations would not have endured if they had no capacity to occasionally serve as important sources and transmitters of catalytic teachings that can dramatically improve a person's experience. If their guidance and advice didn't continue to elicit at least a trickle of fresh new "success stories" and persuasive testimonials, they would have died out as organizations long ago. For all their faults, the well-established religions of the world *do* manage to help at least some of their followers develop and live into more satisfying belief systems. No doubt, there are empowering and liberating beliefs embedded in what they advocate and teach, even if those beliefs are difficult to recognize when obscured by excessive ritual and dogma.

Remember: When considering beliefs advocated by religious organizations, look for beliefs that have all three of these attributes:

- survived the test of time in the experience of others
- resulted in exemplary lives you intrinsically respect and find attractive as models for your own life
- generated numerous passionate and heartfelt personal endorsements

These beliefs are far more likely to lead to a state of mind you desire and enjoy than any beliefs that don't meet these criteria.

**Other sources of guidance**

For those who have difficulty with religious and/or spiritual teachings, there is a large body of completely *non-religious* writing that also gives advice on how to be successful and happy. It's called *wisdom literature*. Some wisdom literature has been around for centuries. For example, *The Way* is thought to have been written by Lao Tzu in China at least four thousand years ago. Ralph Waldo Emerson, Henry David Thoreau, and other transcendentalist were important authors of American wisdom literature in the 19ᵗʰ century. Thoreau's *Walden* in particular has been a profound source of comfort and guidance for many who find it as relevant today as ever. Other sources are much more recent. Stephen Covey (1932-2012) was a professor of business at Utah State University when he decided to use his sabbatical to make a comprehensive survey of American wisdom literature, i.e., advice for living effectively, by some of America's most well-known voices: Thomas Jefferson, Henry David Thoreau, Benjamin Franklin, Abraham Lincoln, Thomas Edison, and others. Covey summarized his findings in his book, *Seven Habits of Highly Effective People*, first published in 1989. The seven habits Covey wrote about support success in both business and personal arenas. His book quickly became a best-seller, and over the years, it has been translated into 40 languages and has sold more than 25 million copies. (That many translations, and that many copies sold constitute an enormous endorsement, so checking out this source is highly recommended.)

There is noticeable and remarkable overlap among the personal values advocated by the world's major religions and the personal values advocated by most of the world's wisdom literature. Whether you consult one of the major religions, or any of the more secular wisdom sources, you're likely to find at least some, if not most, of the following values being advocated as part of a belief system that will help you find and enter your most preferred version of heaven.

1. Love – This is a personal discipline of perceiving and acting in respectful acknowledgment that any living form you encounter – plant, animal, or human – in its most essential core is always in the process of doing its best to express the most authentic and complete version of itself that it can. "Acting in respectful acknowledgment" of that process means you choose words and actions – or sometimes it's stillness and silence you'll choose – that honor, support, encourage, affirm, and celebrate that process as much as you possibly can. It also means that you stick to this discipline, regardless of whether the person or thing you love returns your love,

ignores you, dislikes you, or even actively hates you and works against you. Love is blind; it may *appreciate* receiving love in return, but it does not allow the presence or absence of love from others to alter its self-determination to *be* as loving as possible toward whoever and whatever it encounters. It's a deeply personal discipline about the kind of energy you will send *out* into your world, regardless of the kinds of energy you receive *from* that world.

2. Respect – This is a quieter version of love as it manifests in less challenging daily interactions.

3. Acceptance – This has to do with the blindness of love. It means that you refrain from judging; you refrain from assigning any sort of negative value to anything you encounter.

4. Patience – This is remembering that sometimes, instead of expending effort to change something, it's better to wait; it's better to allow that thing to change on its own, in its own time. Here's the corollary: Being "in a hurry" a*lways* lowers the experiential quality of the time you spend "being in a hurry."

5. Presence -- Reminiscing about the past, and enjoying fantasies about the future can be entertaining, but neither is capable of delivering the full intensity of fulfillment that living in the present provides. Presence is knowing that *this* moment – right *now* – is your *only* opportunity to soar, to *live* in your own most preferred version of your own most personal heaven.

6. Generosity – Constant willingness to share from whatever resources you have. It helps greatly to have a strong assumption of abundance – the idea that you will always have enough of whatever you need.

7.  Openness – Consistently refusing to judge, categorize, compartmentalize, label, or otherwise limit the reality of anything new that appears in your experience. Your mind instinctively tries to judge, categorize, and compartmentalize, because those are its ways of making sense of anything new you encounter, and keeping you safe from any threat that might be lurking. It takes discipline to resist this instinctive temptation, but the rewards make it a worthy and satisfying discipline.

8.  Vision – the practice of maintaining an imaginary version of a future you desire, and the discipline of using that imagined version of your future as the reference point by which you steer the course of your life in the present and into the future.

9.  Hope – Choosing to believe – even when there may not be any evidence at all, and even when the available evidence says "No!" – that what you want *can* and *is* becoming real.

10. Determination – The capacity to continue working to achieve a goal or fulfill a vision you've set for yourself, no matter how much resistance you encounter, and no matter how many times you fail along the way. Ben Franklin and Abe Lincoln both suffered numerous failures during the early years of their careers. In 1962, Nelson Mandela was sentenced to life in a prison, where the only way he could continue fighting to end apartheid was writing letters. Nevertheless, he refused to surrender his determination to end apartheid. Twenty-seven years later, he was released, and became the first black president of South Africa.

11. Self-discipline – You live in a biological meat sack called "your body." Because it is a biological entity, it is subject to all the same biological imperatives as any other life

form. It needs food, water, shelter, and occasional rest. It is also driven to ensure perpetuation of its genetic lineage by mating and reproducing. Moreover, because it's human, it has an ego with an insatiable appetite for every form of gratification imaginable. Self-discipline enables you to manage, moderate, and appropriately direct your otherwise relentless pursuit of gratification on all of these biological and ego-related fronts.

12. Simplicity – "'Tis a gift to be simple." The essence of life is not complicated: the four basic elements are food, water, shelter, and the comfort of feeling safe, connected, and belonging with people you love and respect. Anything more is seen by some as unnecessary complication. Too much complication tends to make life more confusing and burdensome. In 21st century western civilization, the level of complication that has become normal and acceptable – some would even say essential – is so multi-layered and complex that we experience an unprecedented suicide rate. Many people in modern cultures today are so overwhelmed and in so much pain from trying to "manage it all," that a growing number choose to end their lives rather than continue the struggle. Keeping your life simple rather than complicated is nearly always helpful.

13. Honesty – Speaking and acting in absolute consistency with your most accurate assessment of the reality of any situation. Dishonesty is intentionally choosing to speak or act otherwise, usually to avoid discomfort or to take unfair advantage at someone else's expense. Dishonesty with self is especially destructive because it can so easily become a frequent habit. *You* know when you're being dishonest; the experience erodes your respect for yourself. Unfortunately, because dishonesty

with yourself is usually private, there's rarely any external consequence when you fail to hold yourself accountable.

14. Integrity – Concisely, this is about ensuring consistency between your words – including the intentions and promises you express to yourself, even if no one else ever hears them – and your actions. It's about developing and maintaining the discipline to follow through and actually *do* whatever you tell anyone – including yourself –you *intend* to do. It's also about making sure *all* of your words and actions are consistent with all the elements of your belief system.

15. Gratitude – This is the mental and emotional discipline of noticing and acknowledging the many contributions your life receives from others. As observed earlier, you came into the world as a helpless infant. For the first few months at least, *everything* that sustained your life was a gift. You did nothing to deserve any of it, and you did nothing to make any of it happen. If you believe that you've pulled yourself up by your bootstraps and made something of yourself without any help from anyone, stop to remember that *someone* taught you about the *possibility* of "making something of yourself." Someone taught you to *recognize* opportunities. Someone taught you about the *possibility* of seizing an opportunity. Someone taught you about working hard, or showed you what working hard looks like. Each of us builds our consciousness on a foundation composed of such gifts – mainly gifts of teaching – from others. Here's another way I like to think of gratitude: "It's the grease the Universe requires to slide its best gifts into your life. There's no way you can put too much of it into the system!" Another helpful way to think about gratitude is remembering to notice that, without it,

your experience of the world will seem mostly flat and two-dimensional, and it will only appear in black-and-white. The more you practice gratitude, the more three-dimensional, bright, and colorful your reality will seem!

**3. Keep in touch** -- Failing to do so would be like sailing over the horizon, out of sight of land, with no compass and no stars by which to steer. As soon as you lose sight of land, you're effectively lost. You can find yourself feeling frighteningly alone, including the feeling that *no one understands* how lonely and lost you feel. Even worse, you can get so disconnected from the consensus reality that when you reach out for help, no one seems to understand that it's help you're asking for. (When no one understands your cries for help, you are *truly* help-less i.e., without help. If that happens, you *are* seriously lost.)

Unfortunately, society often perceives an individual who has become radically disconnected from the prevailing belief system as "insane." (Ironically, an "insane" person usually believes with total sincerity that what he or she is saying and doing makes perfect sense.) If an insane person is having a rough time and sincerely reaches out for help, the lack of continuity between belief systems can be so extreme that the people who hear that cry for help perceive it as an indication of insanity. If it's too far outside their realm of familiarity, they may become fearful. They may alert authorities to arrest and incarcerate the "insane" person in a mental institution. If that happens, the "insane" person is likely to be subjected to heavy doses of mind-altering drugs. Again, not pretty. So be careful, consult guidance resources often, and make sure to stay in touch.

**4. Don't be afraid to ask for help** – Dysfunctional consciousness can be extremely self-defeating. There is abundant evidence that some people find themselves entangled in internal challenges that repeatedly produce less-than-desirable realities, limited by endless friction, resistance, and other apparent obstacles. The enigmas of depression and bi-polar disorders are well known, but not well understood. External challenges, such as sudden severe trauma – including extremely frightening experiences, even if there was no actual injury or pain – can leave chronic and debilitating fears. Physical, psychological, and/or emotional abuse can do tremendous psychological and emotional damage. Just one of these challenges can severely compromise a person's ability to maintain a positive self-image, enter close relationships, experience love, or cultivate the self-discipline necessary to hold a job and manage the responsibilities of living independently. A person burdened with two or more may find it impossible to manage as an individual without continuous support and assistance. Even simple neglect can result in a compromised belief system. (As we said earlier, during infancy through childhood, everyone absorbs a belief system from his or her caregivers. In cases of severe neglect, the belief system simply may not have developed enough to support a fulfilling experience of *any* reality.) Science is still searching for reliable ways to address the most severe manifestations of dysfunctional belief systems.

If you find yourself trying to make adjustments in your belief system, but it seems unresponsive to your best efforts, consider this analogy. If you're trying to manage a long rope, you may find yourself dealing with a tangle that *seems* like a hopeless knot — seemingly endless loops around other seemingly endless loops. The more you pull on either end, the worse the tangle becomes and the tighter the "knot" seems to become. However, sometimes, if you pause to look carefully, you find it's *possible* to extend the rope to its full length *without* passing either end through any loop, but first, you have to figure out which loops are encircling other loops. Usually, when every loop is empty, you can pull the rope out to its full length. However, figuring out the conflicting loops in your own belief system is never easy and can seem impossible. Einstein said it best: a problem cannot be solved by the same level of consciousness that created it. This is where a skilled counselor can be hugely helpful. A counselor is trained to listen from an outside perspective that is *not being compromised by* the belief system that's experiencing the difficulty. Psychology, psychiatry, social work, and religion/spirituality all have their counseling methodologies for helping people work out the tangles in their personal belief systems. If you find yourself having difficulty adjusting your belief system, seeking help from a professional counselor can be a very smart and helpful move.

## One more important reason to manage your beliefs

Unless you successfully complete these two steps
- Identify and purge your dysfunctional beliefs
- Establish a strong core of reliable and fully functional beliefs in their place

the public discourse may often seem like an extremely intense storm with violent winds and huge crashing waves. You may even feel desperate, sometimes, for *some*thing – *anything* – secure and stable enough to trust for safety. You probably won't find it in the public discourse, because most of those voices are not interested in your well-being or your desire to soar in your life. Many of those voices attempt to attract followers by undermining whatever confidence you might have in other voices. It can seem like a maelstrom of

"Don't believe *her*, don't believe *him*, believe *me!*" *and "This* is the *one-and-only, real, inside* truth." For someone being tossed about in this confusing cacophony, with no stable core of beliefs from which to make decisions about *who* to believe or *what* to believe, the comfort (and drama) of believing that you've tuned into a special "insiders only" kind of "truth" can be seductive. This is the allure of conspiracy theories. Be wary.

# Closing thoughts on learning to fine-tune your belief system

Here's a an example of how free it's possible to be: A friend who grew up as the son of a missionary in a small town in Costa Rica once told me a story about a man there who was convinced he was a bus. Every morning, this man would get up early and strap on a belt that had a vehicle license plate hanging from it in the back (so that he looked at least *a little bit* like a vehicle as he made his way down the street.) Right on schedule each morning, he would jump out in the traveling lane of the town's main street and start running along, exactly *as if* he were a bus. At each designated bus stop, he would slow to a stop near the curb, make a sound with his mouth to simulate the noises of compressed air opening the doors on a real bus, and make a distinctive mechanical looking motion with his arm. That motion would stop with his arm fully extended toward the curb at chest height. His "door" was open, and at the end of his arm, he would be holding a small cup in his hand, directly in front of the real passengers who were waiting for the real bus. Inevitably, one or two of them would put a few coins in his cup. At that point, he would make the appropriate compressed air sounds and movements with his arm to "close his door." Then he would run along to the next stop where he would repeat the process. More and more people would put more coins in his cup. This man who *believed* he was a bus would do this every day, and once or twice a week, he would even run over the mountain to the next town, just like the actual bus. He didn't cause any problems for his neighbors or the local authorities. He was polite to his "passengers." He collected enough money to feed and clothe himself, so he was not a financial burden on anyone. This man who believed he was a bus was tolerated – if not *welcomed!* – for the refreshingly playful absurdity of his beliefs and the whimsical color he added to the life of his community!

# Attention

*Managing where and how you spend your*
*attention is the second step in learning to soar.*

Notice that whenever you're awake, you're *always* paying attention to *some*thing *some*where. The focus of your attention is either in the external environment around you, or in your internal environment, which includes the internal dialogue you experience as "self-talk," as well as physical sensations, memories, fantasies, plans, responsibilities, "to-do" lists, and everything that arises from your own imagination. The focus of your attention can lift you up, or it can bring you down. Managing your attention is about learning to intentionally choose content that lifts you up and moves you toward the reality you want most. It's also about learning to "steer around" the content that brings you down.

Everybody is familiar with the words "pay" and "spend." We use those two words all the time when talking about money. Unless you have a lot of money, you're probably careful about where and how you spend it. You probably try hard to make choices that give high value for your money, and preferably, enduring value. You know that in the long run, if you spend your money carefully and strategically over time, you'll probably be able to accumulate some modest reserves at least, and maybe even some actual wealth. It's the same with attention. Try to start thinking in terms of "spending" your attention. If you develop strong habits about being careful where and how you *spend* your attention i.e., choosing content that lifts you up as often as possible, you'll find yourself moving into a much richer experience of reality.

A "richer experience of reality" is actually the end result most people are longing for when they dream of financial wealth. It's not the exotic high-performance car they really want. It's the *feeling* they imagine they would feel if they owned such a car and could drive it anytime they want. It's not the big fancy house they really want. It's the *feeling* they believe they would experience if they owned and lived in the big fancy house. Unfortunately, when imagining the attractive possessions which people believe would lead to a richer experience of living, most people fail to include in their fantasies what I call "the burdens of ownership." Whether you buy a small and simple car that's inexpensive to operate and easy to maintain, or a big fancy car, (which will probably require more frequent repairs,) and whether you buy a small and simple house, or a big fancy house, there will be associated burdens of ownership. In each case, there will likely be financing costs, insurance premiums, monthly operating expenses, routine maintenance, and occasional major repairs (which can require considerable time for locating and selecting acceptable contractors, and considerable money to pay them when the work is done.) Notice that the burdens which come with a big fancy car are much larger than the corresponding burdens for a small and simple car. The burdens which come with a big fancy house are much greater than their corollaries for smaller and simpler home. Some level of "burden of ownership" is part of what you are buying with nearly every tangible possession you purchase, from the simplest device, like a coffee maker, to a much more complicated and sophisticated appliance, such as an expensive digital clothes washer equipped with multiple settings allowing you to choose from among 62 possible cycles. (Ask yourself: Once you've become accustomed to the new machine, how many of those cycles will you actually use on a regular basis?). Most people fail to acknowledge these "burdens of ownership." Nevertheless, the more material possessions you acquire, especially if you have expensive tastes and want a large number of complicated possessions, the more you'll find yourself diverting valuable time and attention to the burdens of ownership those possessions bring. Time and attention spent on burdens of ownership actually take you *away* from that "richer experience of living" you're seeking.

Most people don't realize that it's possible to enjoy "a richer experience of reality" simply by steering your efforts much more directly toward the *feelings* you want to experience, rather than being distracted by the sparkly objects and upscale possessions you imagine will give you those feelings. As you watch your attention shift from one focus to another, you can notice corresponding shifts in your feelings and how your experience of reality improves or deteriorates with each shift. You'll soon realize that each focus of attention produces its own unique feeling. You can begin to recognize the categories of subject matter for your focused attention that give you experiences of reality that are rich and fulfilling, and the categories that leave you feeling less than satisfied. Learning to carefully manage where and how you spend your time and attention can enable you to move much more directly to the feelings you desire. This strategy can also be quicker, easier, and more likely to lead to success. One other nice benefit is that this strategy produces noticeable improvements as soon as you begin using it!

Developing discipline about where and how you spend your time and attention is not easy. As noted in Chapter 1, the public discourse is almost always blaring unhelpful and insidiously invasive messages, often in the form of advertising. The pervasive and incessant drumming of these messages is what seduces many into stretching their budgets to the max to make extreme purchases like the fancy car or the big house mentioned in previous paragraphs. (That "stretched budget," is also stressful, requiring its own expensive anesthetics, such as the best scotch, the deluxe cable TV package, etc.) Unless you give yourself significant breaks in natural settings – with all devices turned "off," so that advertising cannot penetrate your awareness -- you are unlikely to escape the onslaught.

The "entertainment" programming delivered by advertising has its own range of challenges to your ability to direct your time and attention most productively toward the life you seek. Admittedly, some of the content in broadcast and print media is legitimate news, documentaries, and displays of athletic ability and genuine talent. All of these can be truly entertaining. However, a surprisingly large part of mass media programming content is nothing more than seductive distraction. It has no redeeming value or usefulness beyond the moments you spend with it. It's actually nothing more than anesthesia for your consciousness. It's considered "successful" if it keeps your mind pleasantly occupied (and distracted from the societal problems which the sponsoring commercial interests don't want you to know about, think about, or do anything about.) The business executives who make the decisions about which programs will be sponsored by their advertising dollars will never support the delivery of programming content that might negatively affect your inclination to consider buying their products or services. An airline will never sponsor a documentary about airplane crashes. A producer of processed foods will never sponsor any program that casts doubt on the nutritional value of processed foods. Although you may not have realized this, even the *content* of the programs you see and hear *between the commercials* is skewed to support commercial interests.

There are still other problems with "entertainment" programming. Much of it is absolutely *not* a productive focus on which to spend *any* of your attention. Take, for example, your average crime show. You watch as a crime is committed, and then as police unravel the clues, or detectives unravel the motives, or attorneys seek and discover details in their preparations for an appearance in court. In each example, what usually makes the program so compelling is the fact that it's intensely filled with personal drama: physical, emotional, and psychological intensity, violence, and pain, and the resulting emotions of fear, anxiety, anger, sorrow, and outrage.

Your experience of watching this kind of "entertainment," may seem completely harmless, but here's why it's not good for your experience of living, and doesn't help you learn to soar: Modern brain research has demonstrated conclusively that what you experience vicariously – i.e., what you imagine -- has almost the same effect as if you *actually* experience it. This effect is so strong that it has been used successfully to train Olympic downhill skiers by having them practice *in their imaginations.* They imagine skiing the course of an upcoming race. They may even watch a video of the course, enabling them to more accurately visualize themselves finding the exact line they'll need to follow. A skier who can "ski the perfect line" every time *in his or her imagination* is more likely to "nail it" when skiing the actual course and is more likely to win the race in actual competition. It's vicarious practice, but it's almost as powerful as actual practice.

The powerful effect of vicarious practice means that when you watch a typical crime show, you are *practicing* – in your imagination, at least – emotional and psychological realities you don't *ever* want to *actually* experience. If you're not seeking the emotional and psychological experiences you participate in vicariously when you watch television drama, if you don't want those experiences to be part of your actual future, then you're working against your own best interests when you spend your time and attention practicing them vicariously. The heroes, victims, and villains in a crime show are rarely presented as people who are soaring. Nothing helpful comes from watching any of them, or imagining – vicariously experiencing -- any of their experiences, as you inevitably do when you watch this kind of programming.

Why does programming filled with so much mental and emotional dissonance – even horror -- become so popular, show after show, season after season? Why do so many people actively and intentionally choose these programs, when there are so many options, when so many far more fulfilling choices are available? These questions are worth some careful consideration, especially considering these facts:

- A huge portion of all television "entertainment" focuses on imaginary characters involved in situations that are rife with unpleasant psychological and emotional energy. More than a few of these programs stop at nothing less than graphic depiction of mental, emotional, and physical violation, including the worst forms, such as murder, rape, war, and terrorism.

- The same observation can be made about a huge portion of the movies shown in theaters and available for rent or streaming on line. "Feel good" stories that leave you with something to feel good about after your viewing experience ends are increasingly difficult to find.

- Video gaming is no different. In fact, much of its content is even more extreme and more densely packed with violent and destructive images and situations that (thankfully) have absolutely no corollary in anyone's *actual* reality. Millions are addicted; they spend untold hours practicing their abilities to function effectively in situations they would never choose for the permanent contexts of their lives. They're practicing for life in realities they don't actually want and will never actually encounter. Meanwhile, since all those hours are *not* being spent in practicing any kind of effective living with real people in real situations, the net effect leaves them less equipped to deal effectively with the real people and real situations they will inevitably encounter.

The answer is drama. Following the theatrical definition, Google's second definition for drama is "an exciting, emotional, or unexpected series of events or set of circumstances." Drama is compelling. It can be mental, physical, emotional, or psychological arousal; it can be two or more, or even all four at the same time.

When you focus your attention on "dramatic" programs, it's important to realize and remember that what you're participating in has been imagined by someone else, who communicated the vision in some sort of script, so that it could be produced, packaged, and made available to you in the form of a book, movie, television show, video game, or other form of media that you consume vicariously for entertainment and/or diversion. You're actually participating in "second hand" reality. You're using your imagination to re-live someone else's vision of a reality they've already imagined or experienced. My term for this kind of "packaged" drama is "pseudo-drama." It's "pseudo," because it's a substitute for the real thing. It's second-hand goods. *Real* drama, in contrast, is the feeling of being in the "whitewater" of living. It's exciting and unpredictable. It's adventure. People enjoy adventure that's intense and unpredictable, so long as they have confidence they're safe.

Authentic realities are so infinitely rich that even the most careful and skillful coding – the writing in a novel or a screenplay for a movie or television production, the script for a theater production, or the storyboard for a video game -- rarely captures more than a small part of the original authentic intensity. Therefore, spending your attention on "pseudo drama" almost never delivers the fullness required for you to experience the intense satisfaction and fulfillment that are the essence of your own personal version of heaven. Pseudo drama may have electrifying sizzle in the moment, but it usually leaves you feeling empty or heavy with no lasting satisfaction.

It probably wouldn't be difficult for you to imagine spending an entire day, just kicking back and enjoying some of your favorite ways to relax. Over a nice slow breakfast with extra coffee, you might watch a morning talk show with news, weather, and interviews with celebrities or other interesting and colorful personalities. (All of the above is punctuated, of course, by glib commentary.) After breakfast, you might catch up on reading your favorite magazines (sports, finance, hobbies, home and garden, whatever you enjoy most.) Listen to some music. Watch highlights from last weekend's activities in your favorite sport. Listen to an updated version of the news, this time including in-depth analysis, predictions, and implications for investors. Switch to your podcasts, and catch up on those. By this time, you've eaten both lunch and dinner while enjoying these other activities. Spend the first half of the evening watching live broadcast of a sporting event that will determine which team advances to the next round of the playoffs. Finish the evening by settling back to enjoy yet another re-broadcast of one of your favorite old movies. Maybe you fall asleep reading a few more pages of that novel you've been trying to finish.

If this fantasy sounds attractive, consider these details, which you probably omitted from your fantasy: At the end of the day, you will have had little or no physical exercise, and little or no meaningful authentic interaction with any real live person in real time. You may have enjoyed being "entertained" all day, but your body will probably feel heavy and a little sluggish. You won't be experiencing any of the satisfaction that comes from performing meaningful work to produce useful accomplishments. And while one day like this, here and there, may seem to be a good thing, it should quickly become obvious that a continuous sequence of days like this could easily lead to a heavy lethargy, and even to depression. In his classic *Small is Beautiful: A Study of Economics As If People Mattered* (1973,) respected British economist E.F. Schumacher noted that meaningful human-scale work nourishes the soul (substitute "heart" or "spirit") in much the same way food nourishes the body. Just as the body atrophies and eventually becomes ill without exercise and appropriate nourishment, your consciousness is subject to atrophy and illness without the nourishment of

- Real interactions with the real world around you, especially nature
- Real interactions with real people in real time
- The satisfaction of real work that produces accomplishments you value intrinsically

Over indulgence in dramatic programming may, in fact, leave you with horrifying internal images that persist indefinitely, even bordering on PTSD. In contrast, when you focus your attention on experiencing nature, interacting with real people, or paying attention to your own imagination, and when you act intentionally with any of these as your source of guidance, the real drama you experience may not be quite so electrifying or sizzling as what you can experience vicariously using media. However, this real drama is satisfying in a deeper and richer way, and it offers far more potential to leave you with fulfilling and satisfying memories that will be much more enjoyable and much more enduring. Pseudo drama, in contrast, leaves you feeling empty and tired; it doesn't help you soar.

Talk to any adult who is regularly and frequently engaged in authentic living — going places, doing real activities, having authentic real experiences, and completing useful accomplishments. It's unlikely that person spends much time on pseudo-drama. People who are "living large" enjoy real drama far more. The opposite is also true: a person who spends a lot of time vicariously participating in dramatic programming – whether it comes from television, movies, video games, or reading material – spends more time in a world of *pseudo-drama*. It seems engaging and entertaining in the moment, but most of it offers virtually no lasting satisfaction or genuine fulfillment. Such people typically don't travel much or enjoy much variety in their actual experiences, and they usually accomplish less and make less progress toward their dreams and ambitions, because pseudo-drama so easily becomes such a time-consuming habit. To a person who rarely experiences the authentic drama of living intentionally, vicariously experienced pseudo-drama is compelling, even addictive. It's not uncommon to hear someone say, "I'm *addicted* to my soaps!"

People can also become addicted to the very real but notably unfulfilling dynamics of inter-personal drama, i.e., problems in the lives of people they encounter. Interpersonal drama is rampant. For many, close family members are easy targets for criticism, judgment, and condemnation for words they have spoken or failed to speak, and actions they have taken or failed to take. The ill-advised actions and omissions of close friends, neighbors and other casual acquaintances, store clerks and office administrative officials, or figures in the news, even though they may live and act in far away places, are also fair game for someone who loves to indulge in interpersonal drama. Parents talk about their children. Supposedly mature adults continue to complain and feel oppressed about things their parents said and did years ago. Some husbands and wives complain about their partners as well as their in-laws. Nearly everyone knows someone at work who is irritating and unpleasant socially, professionally, and/or politically, because they tend to go on endlessly about irrelevant personal drama. Often referred to as "gossip," this kind of interpersonal conversation, whether you're the speaker or the listener or both, is unfulfilling. It doesn't feel uplifting while you're in the middle of it, and it does nothing to help your day go better after it's over.

Drama about self is even worse. "Crying the blues" consumes untold hours and rarely yields any redeeming value. Most of us have experienced being drawn into the "poor oppressed me" ranting of someone who perceives himself or herself as a victim. Sometimes, the cause is legitimate bad luck. More often, it's the consequence of poor choices driven by one or more dysfunctional beliefs. Even a minor inadvertent slight can cause such a person to take offense and start "crying the blues." It's true that nearly everyone sometimes makes seriously hurtful and destructive choices, some knowingly, some naively. But for those addicted to interpersonal drama, even the slightest affront seems to justify endless ranting to anyone who will listen. When a victim's lament includes liberal doses of venomous judgment and blame, the experience becomes toxic for speaker and listener alike, and further expands the amounts of time and attention wasted.

Many people also make a habit of "crying the blues" about their sense of inadequacy or loneliness, and the ineffectiveness and lack of success they experience in their lives. Most listeners are unwilling to absorb more than a few doses of these kinds of interpersonal drama. When you recognize a person's propensity for this kind of interpersonal drama, you're more likely to avoid that person, choosing instead to spend your time with more interesting people. Of course, this adds to the sense of loneliness and isolation for the one who is lonely or ineffective, so no good comes to anyone from this kind of drama.

Interpersonal gossip is never a good focus on which to spend your attention and time. Participating in this form of drama, whether you're the speaker or the listener, may *seem* "entertaining" in the moment, but it's not actually fulfilling on any level and not helpful for the future. In fact, participating in the counter-productive dynamics of interpersonal drama is a form of practice that has the same negative impact as watching pseudo drama on television. It only makes more of the same more likely in your future.

Yet another form of unhelpful drama is worth noting, and it too, has become rampant: conversations in which the participants play "ain't it awful," or "I really hate it when . . ." News about the most recent happenings in political, economic, and environmental arenas is full of dynamics that can easily trigger outrage. In recent years, there has been an explosion in the popularity of conspiracy theories, which fuel the same kinds of pointless conversations and drama. Unfortunately, many people form highly charged emotional opinions about whatever content they absorb from the public discourse. That content may be factual and accurate, or it may be pure fabrication. Either way, it can become the fodder of intense drama. Some people spend untold hours obsessing about what's happening, how and why it's happening, and asserting their opinions about who is to blame and what ought to be done to improve the situations. More often than not, the villains in this category of drama are usually so far away, and their actions or inactions so remote, that there is actually no discernible local effect on the participants in these conversations. Those who participate in these conversations fail to realize that the content they find so animating is usually *just a story,* which may or may not be accurate and is probably impossible to verify. Though highly animated and full of drama, most of these conversations are almost entirely pointless. Participation leaves you feeling drained far more often than it lifts you up. If you feel strongly about something that's going on, do a little research and find some way to take constructive action. Ranting endlessly to whoever will listen does you no good. It's not pleasant or helpful to your listeners, either. If you encounter someone trying to play this game, save yourself some time: politely excuse yourself and move along toward a more redeeming focus for your attention.

The most absurd form of pseudo drama that can easily steal your valuable and attention, is news from the worlds of professional sports and professional entertainment. It's true that watching actual sporting events, or enjoying actual performances of legitimate talent is healthy entertainment. What's not healthy is spending your time and attention on discussion and analysis of what has already happened in these arenas, and opinions and speculation about what is likely to happen.

Both radio and television now offer multiple regularly scheduled programs that are exclusively filled with this kind of content. Entire magazines now focus on such news from a single sport, or a single sector of the entertainment world.

The public discourse frequently puts star athletes and entertainers on pedestals. It examines every aspect of their personal lives, which have little or nothing to do with their success as athletes or performers. Do you really care whether this athlete was responsible for a fender-bender in some far away city, or if that actor threw a tantrum and walked off the set? Is an opinion about what makes a successful marriage or how to raise children more important or more worthy because it's spoken by a celebrity athlete or entertainer? And should anybody outside the celebrity's immediate circle have access to personal details such as marital infidelity, problems with addiction or other neuroses, or challenging health issues? It's almost unbelievable, but there's at least one entire magazine devoted to the characters and pseudo-dramas unfolding in television soap operas. People who read such content are wasting valuable moments of their lives on *pseudo-drama about pseudo-drama*. Time and attention spent on this kind of pseudo drama is wasted time.

Broadcast news is yet another source of unhealthy drama. If you feel that you really need to "follow the news" to "be a responsible person," here's a reminder of two highly useful tips (already covered in more detail in Chapter 1.)

1. *Reading* your news from print sources enables you to manage its impact more effectively to make it less damaging to your consciousness. At least when you read, you can hear the words internally in your own voice with your own sense of seriousness and importance. Feelings

of fear are not thrust upon you by a radio or television personality who is functioning as an actor as much as a journalist. You can decide for yourself what level of concern is warranted.

2. If you decide the article you're reading is not worth your attention, you can stop mid-sentence and move on to a different article. *Reading* the news enables you to make better decisions about how you're spending your attention.

Next, let's consider television game shows as a possible focus of your attention. Their appeal is the vicarious but totally unrealistic experience of getting something for nothing – fantastic prizes for solving silly puzzles, answering trivia questions, or even making choices as random and empty as selecting the right treasure chest from a "million dollar pyramid." Vicariously participating in such a program makes you *less* effective in getting what you want in life, because during all the time you're watching, you're spending your attention *vicariously practicing* totally unrealistic strategies that will never help you obtain or achieve *any*thing.

Whatever you select as the focus of your attention *becomes your reality* for as long as you give it your attention. As you watch your attention shift from one focus to another, you can begin to notice and recognize corresponding shifts in your feelings and how your experience of reality improves or deteriorates with each shift. You'll begin to realize that each focus of attention produces a different feeling. By paying close attention to patterns in your experience, you can learn to make far more satisfying choices far more often. Unless you develop considerable discipline about what you allow to become the focus of your attention, your experience of reality is probably hijacked more often than you realize.

Any form of media which you allow to become the focus or your attention becomes the software your imagination runs to generate a vicarious reality. You pay attention, and the focus of your attention guides your imagination into giving you vicarious experiences of the realities that make up its content. Media can guide you into vicarious experience that are entertaining, educational, uplifting, and/ or inspiring, but it's just as effective at guiding you into experiences you would never choose in real life – interpersonal violence, wanton destruction, and horrible mental and emotional states.

*Take control of where and how you spend your attention. Be extremely careful about how much you vicariously practice any reality which you wouldn't want to routinely experience.*

All media sources have one thing in common: they *mediate* the content they deliver. As you read or watch or listen, you fall into the illusion that what you're experiencing is real, or as good as real, when in fact, it's all infused with the values and perspectives of the people who imagine, write, produce, and/or deliver the content you're consuming. Media content is the "bait" that draws you in, so that you become the willing and compliant audience for the sponsors' advertising messages.

Media programming takes you *away* from the here and now where your *real* life is *actually* happening. The reality you most want to live in – your own personal version of heaven – will almost never come to you through media, because your real life originates deep in your own consciousness. It will come from your own authentic imagination, or from nature, or from being out in the world doing real activities and interacting with real people in real time and real space – not through media or in cyberspace. Media can provide fine diversions. Each form of it offers great options when you need to "take a break" from the work of living intensely. Think of choosing to indulge in media the same way you might think of enjoying a glass of wine or a cold beer. In moderation, it can be delightfully pleasant. Over-indulgence can lead to addiction, which is usually progressive and often destructive in the long run.

Wean yourself from your media habit. Instead, cultivate the habit of spending your attention in *every* situation looking for the reality you would *most* like to be living in. If you want to "make the world a better place," if you wish the world could be at peace and "live as one," you don't have to join the Peace Corps and go half way around the world for two years. You don't have to take vacation days from work and spend a lot of money to go on an international mission trip. You don't have to work for a non-profit, or even get involved in organized politics. Opportunities to make the world a better place are all around you every day. Simply dare to relate to the person who is selling you that cup of coffee as if he or she has been a dear friend for years. Let your most warm and welcoming energy flow with that person, and with anybody and everybody you encounter. Do your best to find beauty and hope in every situation.

If you find yourself in a situation that seems barren, find some beauty or hope *inside yourself* and then find a way to project *that* into the situation. Let *that* be your contribution toward making that barren situation more like your ideal world. If you're alone, take the time to do *whatever you're doing* with as much grace and beauty and love as you can possibly bring to it. Do it as if it will be the last act of your life, so that if you have to look back on it from some "next dimension," you'll be able to say to yourself, "I ended on a really good note." You'll be amazed at how dramatically these simple shifts in attitude and behavior can transform even the most mundane and boring activities. Remember: You always have the power to choose how you will relate to any situation. Using the power of will and choice, you can bend almost any situation toward your own personal version of the heaven you desire.

Time is another factor to be clear about as you learn to manage how you spend your attention more carefully. It's easy to get distracted from the present by spending your attention and focusing your imagination on the future. If you do that with a positive and/or hopeful attitude, the result is called fantasy or daydreaming. This can be satisfying and entertaining when you need a break. However, if you imagine your future with a negative or fearful attitude, we call that pessimism or worry. Either way, these are choices you can make about how you spend your attention and use your imagination *in the present* to give yourself an entertaining, but *vicarious* experience. And because imagining the future produces a *vicarious* reality, it's a *pseudo*-reality that cannot yield any *lasting* satisfaction or fulfillment. Be careful to make good choices about which realities you allow to become the focus of your attention. And remember that "your future" really only exists as images in your imagination *as it is functioning in the present*. Fantasies of your future always *happen* right here, right now, in the *present* moment.

Almost all of the same observations can be made about your past. Most people tend to think of "the past" as a real thing composed of memories of real events, experiences, and feelings. But like "the future," your "past" doesn't exist anywhere except in your own imagination as you experience it vicariously by remembering – calling memories to mind and letting those memories guide your imagination -- in the present. Yes, you can look around in the present and find real evidence those historical events actually *did* happened, and that you really *did* have those experiences. You can look at old photographs and read historical accounts. That evidence *is* real. And yes, those events *were* real *at one time*, but that time is gone. They aren't real *now*. Spending attention on "your past" is using your imagination *in the present* to vicariously re-play those memories. Remembering is a choice you make about how you spend your attention *in the present*.

As with "your future," you can vicariously enter the world of your memories with a positive attitude, or a negative attitude. If you take a positive attitude, you'll probably experience warmth and satisfaction. That can be enjoyable the same way a great book, or a good movie can be entertaining or even reassuring. You can also go into your memories with negative attitudes, which can result in vicarious experiences such as anger, pain, regret, sorrow, and/or guilt. Spending your attention re-living unpleasant memories can be almost as unpleasant as the original experiences. Instead of re-living embarrassment or regret over mistakes you made in the past, try learning to look at who you were in those memories with gentleness and forgiveness, i.e., with compassion. Beating yourself up in the present over an unpleasant memory from the past is never a good way to spend your time and attention, especially if you've already beat yourself up more than enough in previous times of remembering it. Remember: even though your memories *seem* to be "in the past," you're actually spending your *present* moments to re-experience them. Even worse, spending your attention on unpleasant memories strengthens and reinforces your capacity to experience more of those same unpleasant feelings in the future. When you indulge in memories of a negative past, you're actually *practicing* for a negative future. Is there any good reason to make such a choice? The past can be a fine place to spend time occasionally when you want a break from the work of living intensely, but like the future, it offers no lasting satisfaction or fulfillment, because it's a pseudo reality. It takes you away from the present – the *only* time in which your life is *actually* happening.

# Imagination

*Reclaiming the power of your imagination
is the third step in learning to soar.*

Think of any reality you can imagine. (Any material object or abstract idea will do. Just pick one.) If whatever you picked doesn't have independent origin and existence in the non-human natural world – i.e., the realm of material, energy, and all life forms other than people – then it originated in someone's imagination, and someone just like you used his or her imagination and creative efforts to rev it up into something you call "real." Somewhere along the line, someone *pretended* it into reality. I realize this is an unusual use of the word "pretend," but consider:

Everything in all of reality – as we know it – fits neatly into one of four distinct realms.

1. **Matter** – All the elements that make up the periodic table, plus all the combinations of those elements.

2. **Energy** – The most obvious and ubiquitous forms are heat and light, which come naturally from the sun and artificially from burning fuels. In addition, there's electrical energy, which occurs naturally as lightning and artificially from a wide variety of electricity generating mechanisms. Beyond these familiar forms of energy, there's an entire spectrum of invisible electro-magnetic radiation, including radio waves, X-rays, etc.

Before any life forms appeared, interactions of matter and energy made up the entire physical universe, with all its dynamics. There were stars and planets, and on our planet, there were land masses, oceans, rivers, volcanoes, ocean currents, and weather systems that included wind, rain, lightning, hurricanes and tornadoes. All this existed before any life forms appeared. These two realms alone – matter and energy – combined to make up an extremely diverse and dynamic reality.

3. **Life** – Today, there is jaw-dropping variety and diversity of life forms, from the simplest fungi and single-cell creatures, through millions of species of complex plants and animals including human beings. All these life forms interact with both the non-living physical material from the first realm as well as the varieties of energy in the second realm. They also interact with a wide variety of other life forms from both the plant and animal kingdoms. The resulting diversity and complexity of elements in these first three realms interacting with each other is almost beyond comprehension.

4. **Civilization** – Overarching and often affecting these first three realms is a distinctly different fourth realm of realities called "civilization." It consists of everything that has ever been imagined and/or created by humans since the beginning of time. That includes everything from the most primitive stone tools, to pots and pans, furniture, art, buildings, vehicles, institutions, governments, electron microscopes, the scientific method, religions, philosophies, metaphysical belief systems, and theories about quantum physics.

Any "new" reality in this fourth realm begins in the moment when it precipitates or crystallizes *out* of what can be conceptualized as an infinite realm of pure undifferentiated potential *into* the imagination of a single person living in the limitations and particulars of time and space. This is how all new realities in the realm of civilization begin. This is the *only* way *any* distinctly human reality *can* begin. If it can be the subject of a thought, and if it doesn't have an impersonal independent beginning in one of the first three realms, then it either crystallized in *your* mind authentically and originally as described above, or it originated this way in *someone else's* imagination, and was then communicated to you.

This distinctly human "reality creating process" may even be the actual source of the supposedly transcendent and/or parallel dimensions about which some people speak, write, and sometimes act. It's not clear whether the conscious entities that supposedly inhabit some of these exotic dimensions are unique life forms originating from a source as exotic as the dimension itself, or simply further manifestations of our uniquely human capacity to create new realities simply by imagining them, believing in them, acting on our beliefs, and persuading others to believe. Either way, it's quite obvious that as more people begin to believe and act as if a newly imagined reality is, in fact, real, the strength of that reality grows and intensifies. A new possibility becomes more real as those who first believe in it persuade others to believe in it. As more and more people invest time, effort, and materials in expression of any belief, that belief becomes increasingly real.

Just as you are free to believe in whatever you choose at any level of intensity and investment you choose, you are also free to imagine whatever you want. How "real" you make the content of your imagination is entirely up to you. It's limited only by your ability to communicate whatever occurs in your imagination and by your persuasive power to enlist others in believing in and investing in your imagined content. There's no consequence for your choices about what you allow to become "real" in your imagination. The only consequence is in the quality of your own experience. There may be consequences for words and/or actions resulting from your imagination, but usually not for simply imagining.

Note that this way of imagining the source of all realities is retroactive and all-inclusive. It applies to itself. It applies to every concept, every observation, and every suggestion offered in this book. Nothing you read here will have any more reality in your world than you give it. If you give a new idea significant amounts of time and attention, it will gradually become more real to you. In contrast, if you imagine it once and forget it soon after, it will no longer exist in your reality.

## Creating new realities

"Everything is created twice." This is true of all distinctly human realities. It's a fairly well known observation. Google it, and you'll get more than 100,000,000 results. Here's how I would explain it: the first creation is when a person imagines a totally new and fresh possibility that has never before been imagined by any other human. It can occur as an image – visual, auditory, kinesthetic, etc. – or as the essential essence of an abstract idea in its simplest form. There are two ways a second creation can happen. The first is when a person invests enough energy to fashion a material manifestation of what has occurred in his or her imagination. For example, a person makes a stone tool, or shapes a clay pot, or writes a story, or paints a picture, or composes a piece of music and writes the notes on paper. The other way a second creation can happen occurs when a person communicates his or her imaginary content well enough that a second person "tunes in" and begins to imagine and believe in the same content. That second person also begins to experience that content as "real."

When a new idea or image first emerges, it is extremely delicate. You could almost say it "shimmers" like a suggestion on a boundary between potential and reality. Its existence is not quite fully established in anyone's reality, but not yet lost back into the infinite realm of pure undifferentiated potential. If the person who first thought of it doesn't give it attention and amplify it into something more substantial, that totally fresh and new idea or image will probably be lost from reality simply by being forgotten. However, one of the characteristics that most distinguishes humans from all other species is that we have the capacity to nurture a simple new idea into a reality that has enduring substance. You can imagine a song, write it, perform it, and record it. You can envision a new building, and erect an enduring material structure – concrete, steel, glass – that will last for centuries. With intentional investment of effort, the most essential minimum of a new reality can be energized and amplified to become "real" to other people on almost any scale imaginable.

Here's a good analogy for that creative process: A skilled indigenous person – or a trained survival expert – can use a bow drill or a flint to produce a glowing ember. That ember can be transferred into a tinder bundle, and with careful application of breath to supply air, it can be nurtured into a flame. That's the most primitive way fire is made, and it's a good metaphor for how all human realities begin. Indigenous villagers can feed fuel and breath to the ember and build it up into a roaring inferno. In the same way, humans can use their imaginations to expand and elaborate on an original idea, and with efforts and materials, they can amplify what started as a "shimmering suggestion of a reality" into an enduring physical reality in time and space.

The scale is almost unlimited. Humans have created everything from objects as simple as a flint cutting tool, to encyclopedias, international corporations, governments that wield almost unimaginable economic, political, and military power, philosophies and religions, pantheons of gods, and imaginary worlds in imaginary dimensions. *All* realities that are uniquely human began with this kind of crystallization – from potential into particulars – that occurred first in one person's imagination, and later as more enduring realities – concrete or abstract – in the material world.

Humans instinctively know this process of developing imagined ideas into realities. As young children, humans start playing with this power spontaneously. Adults call it "pretending." Think back to your own early childhood, and you'll probably remember something similar to this: When we were just four or five years old, my sister and I would ask our mother to throw a bedspread over a card table, and we would crawl under it, into this newly defined space. With our imaginations, we could transform that space into a house, a school, or a hospital. With intention and will, we could use our imaginations to make the simplest physical suggestion of an imagined reality into something that seemed "real" enough to be entertaining for hours. With my friends from the neighborhood, we could make almost any reality we could imagine out of almost nothing. We pretended that the cardboard carton from the neighbors' new refrigerator was a submarine. By pretending, we transformed an odd assortment of unused furniture and miscellaneous storage boxes we found in a remote corner of the basement into a fort where we played for days. I remember a time when my buddies and I used our imaginations to transform a neighbor's landscaping terrace into a sailing ship. From the "deck" of that "ship," we spent hours fighting off "sea monsters" and "pirates," and harpooning "whales." Many times, we rescued each other from "drowning" in the "tempestuous sea" of grassy lawn. Imagination is powerful stuff! With intentional application of will and the barest suggestion of appropriate physical resources, children regularly transform the contents of their imaginations into powerful and compelling experiences that function for them as "realities."

Adults are obviously bigger, stronger, smarter, and able to control and direct more resources than children. When adults want to make something they have imagined into a reality, they can bring more to the process by organizing the investment of far more resources. Instead of being limited to card tables and bedspreads, capable adults can organize and direct huge amounts of financial resources, physical materials and sophisticated human energy and talent to design and fabricate real objects, construct real buildings, and develop real organizations. Instead of "pretending" a school under a card table, today's adults can organize the construction of real buildings and hire real teachers. But it wasn't always so. Consider the concept of public schools. The original ideas have been grown and developed over many centuries. Today's reality of a "public school system" began in an ancient past when no version of any kind of formal educational system had yet been imagined. Every aspect of a modern public school system had its original beginning in *someone's* imagination:

- buildings with classrooms in which the teachers and students work
- furnishings and textbooks appropriate for the subjects and learning activities

- qualified teachers
- curricula for training teachers
- universities in which to train them
- school boards to hire them
- buses to transport the students
- taxes to provide the resources needed to pay for all of the above

Every element of every bullet point began when someone first imagined the conceptual "seed" of it. Since that beginning, people have planned and invested attention and material resources, and caused each imagined "seed" to grow and develop into the very real features that exist in today's version of a typical public school system.

Even large, complex, and venerable institutions such as universities, religious organizations, corporations, and even entire countries -- can be thought of as large, complicated, and elaborate games of imagination. They're built upon vast networks of agreements about how creative energy may be expressed in high-powered adult processes of willfully and powerfully imagining, believing, and creating realities. Those agreements also specify the imaginary rules, regulations, and conceptual constructs the players will acknowledge, respect, and relate to as "real."

Consider two countries -- the United States and Canada – and the boundary they share. Most of us have seen this boundary line on maps so many times that we comfortably accept it as real. Now go out into the woods and fields try to find it. Except in the facilities at a border crossing. you won't find anything resembling a line. Long segments of that "line" have no physical manifestation at all. We *assume* the existence of it *as if* it has physical reality, but mostly it doesn't. The same is true for boundaries between provinces, states, counties, cities, and towns all over the world. In each case, the boundary line on a map actually represents an agreement about agreements: "On *this* side of this imaginary line, we agree to imagine a reality in which we follow *our* rules and *our* laws. We agree to respect the fact that on *that* side of the line, you have your own agreements defining a different reality, using different rules and different laws which you have imagined and agreed to believe in and play by. You have a game you're imagining on that side of the line, and we're imagining and playing a different game on our side."

It would be fair to say that the reality of any modern nation is actually an extremely elaborate game of imagining. Consider the United States of America as an example. There was a time – think pre-Columbus -- when its reality had not yet been imagined by anyone. The USA began its evolution toward its current reality when a few colonists imagined a new and different game in which they would no longer be required to deal with British rules, regulations, and taxes. They began to talk about what they imagined, and gradually developed a collective vision of a new country that would be independent of Great Britain. This vision grew as more and more people shared it and imagined it as a desirable reality.

Eventually, people began to invest in this vision, and a few began to act as if it were already real. The colonists' growing commitment to this alternative vision eventually led to armed conflict, i.e., the Revolutionary War. People were fighting for the right to drop out of one imagined game – the British Empire – to play a new and different game, which became the United. States. Following victory in the Revolutionary War, a handful of respected colonists got together in Philadelphia and went to work imagining and designing a new government they hoped would be free of most of the problems and limitations they had experienced under British rule. They described and specified their vision in a document we now know as the Constitution. It defined the rules by which the new game would be imagined and played. It even specified rules for changing the rules! Based on that way of thinking about the beginning, it's reasonable to think of the United States of America as a giant game of imagining which people have been playing for more than 250 years. It has seen countless investments of creativity, time, money, hard work, and determined loyalty by millions of people over many years. Their continuing investments build on this legacy to give it all the reality it has.

The United States of America is the same as any other game of imagining in one important way: it could all be transformed into an entirely different game *if* enough of the players could agree on a new game based on new rules. With a small group of children, changing the game by changing the rules is relatively easy. A pretend fort under a card table can become a pretend hospital as quickly as the children playing the game agree to make the shift. With a nation of more than 330 million people and 250 years of investments and traditions, changing the game is a much more complicated proposition. The game has evolved, and the rules have changed somewhat, but thinking of it as a giant and extremely elaborate and complicated game of imagining works perfectly well. People all over the world participate in the game by agreeing to acknowledge and relate to it as real. Their agreement to *imagine together* that it's real is what *makes* it real.

If you really want to escape rational captivity and learn to soar in your life, it's important to recognize that many of the stable and enduring realities you have always believed in are actually giant games of imagination, being played by highly intelligent and resourceful adults. Here's another example that may be helpful: Think about live theater on Broadway. Actors are on stage in costumes appropriate for the time and place as imagined by the author and specified in the script. Sets, furniture, and props are also present, and they are as consistent as possible with the vision the author imagined. The actors wear make-up under bright lights to further emphasize the "realism" of the characters they are portraying. There may even be sound effects from off-stage to simulate the "reality" that's defined in the script. All of this is done to make it as easy as possible for the audience to focus their attention and use their imaginations to enter the pseudo-reality of the play when it is performed. Note that we say the characters "play" their parts. It's all done at a much more elaborate and sophisticated level of "playing" than what we could bring to the games we pretended as children, but it's essentially the same process. The actors pretend to be the characters in the script, creating a pseudo-reality which audience members can enter and enjoy vicariously. The best actors are those who can deliver the most convincing portrayals of their scripted parts. The best plays are those that depict the most convincing vicarious realities.

With live theater, there's one major difference. Unless it's improvisational theater, there's an author somewhere who imagined the pseudo-reality and wrote the script. When we were playing as little kids, we had no script. We used our imaginations, and we called it "pretending." Now, as adults, it makes sense to think of "normal reality" as a much more elaborate, dynamic, and permanently ongoing production of improvisational theater. Shakespeare said this: "All the world's a stage..." However, in "real life," there's no script — only broad consensus on the rules of the game. You're making up your part as you go along. I'm making up my part, and so is everyone else. We all base our choices on who we want to be or feel like being in the moment, what we'd like to experience in the game and from the game in the future, and what the other actors are imagining, saying, and doing.

It's not an exaggeration to say that this is what people actually mean when they say, "everyone creates their own reality." *Whatever vision of your life* you allow to become the object of your focused attention becomes the subject matter for your imagination. As soon as you allow your focused attention to settle on this vision, your imagination automatically goes to work, and with sufficient infusion of time, energy, and materials, *imagines* that vision into what you experience as "reality." It's similar to movie film rolling through a projector: whatever you focus on is the film, your mind is the mechanism of the projector, and your imagination is the projection light. Guided by your attention and your imagination, and with enough creative effort, your mind projects a 3-D "movie" all around you, which you experience as your reality.

Imagining a vision of your own life into reality in this way is what makes your life seem real. When you're actively and intentionally choosing the focus of your attention, you call that "paying attention." When you're being less intentional about where you allow your attention to focus, you say your mind is wandering. You might also call it "daydreaming." When you dream at night, it's as if your imagination is almost completely shut down with only a trace of activity continuing. When your body returns to being fully awake, your capacity to intentionally imagine your life into reality intensifies exponentially. That's why waking reality seems so much more vivid, solid, and convincing than your dreams. You could actually think of "being awake" as dreaming with your intention and attention fully focused and your imagination operating on full power.

Your identity – who you *think* you are now and the life you are *imagining* and trying to live into – exist primarily in your imagination. If you find this concept difficult, list the four or five aspects of your current identity that seem biggest, most important, and most undeniably "real" in your present and immediate future. Then, remember that in vastly different cultures in other parts of the world, there are very different people living very different lives: hunter-gatherers in the Brazilian rain forest, subsistence fishermen in Indonesia, nomadic herders in Mongolia, and Aborigines in the Australian outback, to name just a few. These very different people are all living full lives with friends and partners and children and ancestors. They celebrate births and mourn deaths with the same feelings as you, but some of the "realities" they might list in response to this question would probably be almost impossible for you to imagine. Some of what you listed as "most important and undeniably real" would have little or no reality for them. You might have listed "serving as President of my children's parent-teacher association." A Mongolian herder would probably have no idea how to imagine or pretend to be in that identity. A young Aborigine man might list "maker of tools for my tribe" as an important aspect of his identity. How would you imagine that identity as your reality?

You're probably not accustomed to thinking this way, because fairly early in childhood, you were probably taught, actively and intentionally, to leave your unique imagination and your power of pretending behind. This process of being taught and learning is called "education," but it makes just as much sense to think of it as an elaborate and protracted indoctrination process that distanced you from your most important creative powers. In place of your authentic and unique imagination and your power to pretend your own ideas into reality, you were

145

systematically taught – and probably rewarded for learning – to subordinate those parts of yourself, so that you could become a fully functional, respectful, and productive player – usually some form of pawn -- in a much larger imagination game which was *already going on* all around you, i.e., your surrounding culture's Big Imagination Game.

If you're like most people, a Big Imagination Game has been going on around you all your life. It has been played with powerful and loyal agreement and participation by millions of people on many levels. You've been taught and coerced in almost every way imaginable into participating in it yourself. You may have been participating in it for so long now that you've lost sight of any alternatives. You may even believe that the "society" around you is an independent "reality" that has nothing to do with anybody pretending or imagining anything.

The actual reality of what's been happening, and what continues to happen all over the world, is not hard to see, once you learn to bring it into focus as huge games made possible and "real" by imagination. People who are heavily invested in a Big Imagination Game tend to become extremely serious about maintaining their Big Games, especially if they've maneuvered themselves into situations in which they are reaping lots of rewards and/or power from the games with very little effort! (Let's call them "Game Masters.") They'll go to almost any extreme to preserve and protect their Games *as they are currently being played* (because those games are delivering huge benefits to them.) In addition, they'll go to whatever measures are necessary to squelch any voices that suggest changing the rules or playing a different game. An extreme example of this is going on today in North Korea. Anyone who questions the rules of North Korea's Big Imagination Game is subject to arrest, imprisonment, torture, and even execution.

This squelching of dissent by Game Masters has happened throughout history. Squelching any voice that suggests the game should be changed was the primary agenda when people like Jesus, Joan of Arc, Sir Thomas Moore, Abraham Lincoln, John F. Kennedy, and Martin Luther King Jr. were assassinated. These historical figures were all charismatic, and they all advocated realities that were different from the Big Imagination Games that were going on around them. In each case, the Game Masters became fearful that, left unchecked, these people might seriously disrupt their well-established Big Games. When the Game Masters were unsuccessful in their efforts to suppress or neutralize the threats those voices posed, they turned to violence to make *sure* those voices were silenced permanently. (This dynamic has been going on since the earliest civilizations, and it's still going on today.)

Big Imagination Games go on in different ways in different cultures all over the world. Seeing it all as huge games of pretend helps to explain why life in China seems so different from life in Kenya, which is different from life in the U.S. Every distinct culture is the manifestation of a different Big Imagination Game with different agreements about what is real and important, and different rules for how the game must be played.

Nearly everywhere you go, there's some version of a Big Imagination Game being played. In most of these games, a few individuals who see and understand what is going on a little more clearly, and who are a little more greedy and a little less compassionate than everyone else, have managed to bend the rules of The Big Game to their own advantage. These are the "power brokers" and Game Masters. They are found most frequently in government, big business, finance, and the legal profession. On a slightly lower tier, most professions have a similar cadre of people who have maneuvered themselves into positions of power and authority over the rules by which participants imagine their respective professions into reality. These people play the role of "priests" in their respective professions, just as officially recognized "priests" play this role in religious organizations. If you need a good example, look at the hierarchy of power that defines and controls the Catholic Church. Any group of people that organizes around a particular focus will, if it becomes large enough, evolve its own "priesthood." Academic disciplines, professional associations, political parties, sports leagues, and even non-profit interest groups as benign as the American Kennel Club all have their "priesthoods," small groups of power brokers who control the rules of their respective games, usually to their own advantage. You can think of the entire tapestry of nearly any 21st century society as layer upon layer and hierarchies within hierarchies of games within games. Within each, a few people "at the top" control the rules for those within their span of influence and control. At the lowest levels, of course, are those who understand the least about how these games are being played. Because they understand least, they experience less freedom, are allowed to exercise less power, and receive less of the benefits of the games than nearly everyone else.

If you're like most people, you've left your imagination and your awareness of your capacity to *imagine* your preferred reality into your actual reality so far behind for so long that today, you probably live in and contribute to whatever Big Game is going on around you *as if* it were the only game in town. You may have fallen into thinking of it as an external reality that exists on its own without any dependence on anyone's imagination. The opposite is actually more true. The *apparent* social and political realities in every civilization, society, nation, state, city, town, and village are *totally* dependent on people who make them real by agreeing to participate in a group process of believing in them and willfully imagining them into reality.

You are free to adjust your belief system, develop careful habits about where and how you spend your attention, and begin playing your own more authentic game of pretend *within* the other larger games going on around you. So long as your creations do not upset any of the games going on around you, and you continue to show proper respect, follow the rules, and fulfill your responsibilities in those games, you can create almost any reality you want in your personal life. You can create a reality in which the world around you feels like your own personal heaven. and in that life, you'll feel like the god of that heaven. You can learn to soar!

---

*Here's a playful little diagnostic that might help you realize just how deeply your capacity for using the power of your imagination may be mired in unnecessary limitations. Allow the following description of a challenging situation to guide your imagination:*

Imagine a huge rabbit, close to three feet long and weighing more than 75 pounds. It has extremely large floppy ears, and its fluffy tail is as big as a soccer ball. Now imagine that this rabbit is sitting up on its hind legs inside a big glass bottle that's about three feet in diameter and almost five feet tall, with the top tapering to an opening that's less than a foot in diameter. The rabbit is desperately pawing at the inside of the bottle. It's obvious he wants out.

Here's your challenge: How can you perform a rescue without breaking the bottle or injuring the rabbit? Give yourself as long as you need to ponder this. *(The answer is in italics at the end of this chapter on page 163.)*

---

> *The third step in learning to soar is re-claiming the*
> *power of your imagination, – i.e., resurrecting your*
> *power to envision intentionally and powerfully.*

There are plenty of books, CD's, videos, and workshops claiming they can teach you how to do this. Many of these new voices refer to "the law of attraction," which asserts that people are capable of using their minds to intentionally attract whatever they want and cause it to actually appear in their realities. This process is sometimes referred to as "manifesting." Apparently, this law of attraction is like the law of gravity. It has always been around and in force, even though we haven't always recognized or understood it clearly enough to use it intentionally. Recent and much more widespread awareness of the law of attraction began with the 2005 publication of a video and a book, both called *The Secret*, produced by Rhonda Byrne. (If you haven't seen it, I strongly urge you to locate it and watch it.)

Meanwhile, here's a brief synopsis: First, *The Secret* describes historical examples and gives quotes from people who have made impressive accomplishments in multiple fields. People as diverse as Leonardo da Vinci, Ben Franklin, and Thomas Edison. (A more recent example would be Steve Jobs.) *The Secret* goes on to present a variety of contemporary examples as well. These examples are followed by a crucial question: what enables these individuals to excel and achieve at such impressive levels? The answer? They know "the secret," i.e., the law of attraction.They understand how to use the natural energies flowing in the dimensions of time and space to manifest — i.e., to cause to become real "here and now" in the present — almost anything they desire. The remainder of the book and video are dedicated to explaining how to both understand the law of attraction and begin using it in your own life to begin manifesting your preferred realities intentionally. Byrne's video and book rely partly on direct, well-known quotations from super-achievers in history, and partly on testimonials from contemporary individuals who are currently accomplishing at comparable levels. With Rhonda Byrne's explanations and even more detailed how-to guidance and advice from Mike Dooley's publications, my understanding of manifesting — using the law of attraction intentionally — boils down to these four basic steps and two corollaries:

***The four basic steps are Envision, Believe, Feel, and Act.
The two corollaries are, "Have an attitude
of gratitude," and "Don't hesitate."***

"**Envision**" means, "*Dare* to envision i.e., intentionally imagine in detail, whatever you want to manifest." Envision *whatever* you would have, already fully present as your reality. (If the notion of envisioning doesn't resonate with you, substitute the word "*declare."*) *Declare* — as if you were speaking to the ultimate source of all realities — that you will inevitably have $X$ (whatever you seek) as your reality, and sooner, rather than later. Make this declaration without any trace of reservation based on what you have always believed is possible (or impossible,) or any hint of a suggestion that you might not be worthy to receive and enjoy what you wish to manifest. Envision with all the same innocence and enthusiasm as if you were a 4-year old, telling Santa what you want (and fully expect!) for Christmas. Details are great for focusing your vision, but take care to avoid becoming attached to details. (Feelings are actually the more critical element (as you'll understand more in the third step.) Envision with detail, but also with detachment. Envision yourself enjoying the desired *qualities* of experience you fully expect, as if the vision is already fully manifested in the material reality around you

**"Believe"** means, "Make a purely willful and intentional decision to *believe* -- in total defiance of any perceived limitations -- that what you're envisioning is *already* real on some level, and you are *already* in the process of finding your way to that reality in your own immediate experience." (Admittedly, this step requires a radical sidestepping of rational captivity, which is why it's so important to understand rational captivity — to whatever extent you might be suffering its limitations — well enough to be able to release yourself from it.) *Dare* to believe with absolutely total conviction. You probably have no idea *how* this manifesting process can be happening. That's OK. You don't need to understand *how*. (In fact, as Mike Dooley repeatedly emphasizes in his teachings on using the law of attraction, *trying to understand how*, or worse, trying to help, distracts from the effectiveness of your believing!) Part of you may try to insist that it *can't* happen, because it would be totally inconsistent with everything you're sure of in the present and everything you've ever experienced in the past. Maybe you don't feel worthy of receiving and experiencing what you're asking for. Set *all* of those kinds of hesitations aside. Focus *all* of your will on daring to *believe* that what you're asking for or declaring is *already* becoming your reality.

When you believe, make your visualization a 3-D movie in which you're the main character who is absolutely delighted with all that's going on! Give your vision all the color, texture, sound, taste, smell, and movement you can imagine. Details are great for helping you move into the feelings you'll need to practice in the third step, but don't allow yourself to become *attached* to the details in your vision. Stay open to the possibility that a totally surprising version of what you're envisioning might actually be even *better* than the best particular version you can imagine. For example, you might envision owning a new red Porsche Boxster convertible, with every available option, and you might envision yourself driving it (and feeling thrilled about how much fun it is,) but take care to remain open to the possibility that there may actually be a *different* high performance automobile you would enjoy owning and driving *even more.* (Maybe you've never heard of this better vehicle; maybe it's not yet available for purchase, but it will be arriving in the market soon,) and *that* car might actually be a *more* perfect car for you! Being less attached to specific details leaves more options for fulfillment.

I try to remember that, out of all the possible ways the future *could* unfold, the chances that it *will* unfold *exactly* as I imagine and hope are infinitely small. It's actually more fun to realize that what you're envisioning is more likely to show up as a surprise: it will probably arrive in a form you never would have expected from a direction you wouldn't have predicted at a time that's more convenient than you ever could have planned.

Another aspect of "visualizing" that's not mentioned often enough is the importance of visualizing *in the present.* If you visualize whatever you're hoping for as something that will occur at some point in the future, you are effectively creating it in *a future reality.* If you visualize it in the future, that's where you're creating it, so that's exactly where it will always stay: in the future. You'll never get to it, and you'll never experience it, because we never live in any future. (Remember: the "future" only exists in your imagination; there is no "future" in the world around you.) Actual living is always in the now. Be sure your visualizations are firmly grounded in the present.

**"Feel"** is the third step in making the law of attraction work for you. Feeling is the emotional energy that amplifies and empowers imagination. The primary purpose of detail in your visualization is to help you rev up the psychological, emotional, and visceral *feelings* you believe you would experience *if* you *were already enjoying* the particulars of your vision. Practice imagining how you will feel *after* what you've envisioned has already become real. Go ahead and do your best to *feel – on every level of your being –* as if what you have envisioned has *already* become real. Feel it with as much intense delight, satisfaction, and fulfillment as you can imagine. Don't be content with the level of feeling you would have if you won a local lottery to benefit a local charity. Pretend you are winning a gigantic lottery that will make you far richer than you have previously dared to imagine! Pretend *that* level and intensity of feeling! The essence of this step is daring to *feel* an intentionally chosen reality, even though the physical circumstances around you offer minimal support for what you are envisioning. This is how my sister and I could transform that bedspread over a card table into a school room or a fort. No doubt, you also knew how to do your own version of this when you were a child. Resurrect the real power of your imagination, and use it to actively and intentionally imagine *whatever you want* into reality. The more you practice, the more effective you'll become!

The fourth step is "**Act.**" No matter how limited or hopeless your current circumstances might seem, dare to envision, believe, feel, and then *act*. Every day, do whatever you can from wherever you are using whatever resources are available. Fill your actions with confidence and belief in your vision, even if there's zero evidence to support your belief. You may have to rely on sheer will power alone and feelings you pretend into reality using only your will and your imagination. No matter how counter-intuitive this may seem, trust the law of attraction. Use that same willpower to disregard any limitations based on lack of resources or prior certainty about what is or is not possible. Take action with full heart and commitment, but also with complete detachment. That means you avoid any kind of attachment to any particular outcomes from your actions. Take any action that might somehow engage, encourage, and support whatever processes you can imagine that *might* be part of your vision becoming real, no matter how remote the connection might seem. This step also requires at least a temporary release from rational captivity. Act with creativity, intelligence, and intention, but remain open and expect to be pleasantly surprised!

Think of whatever actions you take as your quiet way of expressing your commitment to your vision. As stated earlier, it's not necessary to know or understand *how* the law of attraction works. In fact, Mike Dooley repeatedly emphasizes that trying to understand *how* — and worse, any effort to *make it happen* — only creates interference that's counter-productive. Dare to trust that taking whatever actions you can every day using whatever resources are available that seem like they *might* be helpful is *all* you need to do.

Manifesting is as simple as practicing these four steps,
1. Envision the reality you seek
2. Believe in that vision (willfully and powerfully)
3. Enjoy the feelings you desire *now* (by using your imagination as powerfully as you can)
4. Act with complete detachment and pure trust

If you practice these four steps regularly, you can relax in knowing you are fully engaging the law of attraction and all of its power. Dare to enjoy trusting that some version of whatever you're envisioning is *already* crystallizing *out* of the infinite realm of pure undifferentiated potential *into* particulars in your reality in time and space! As stated earlier, your vision may manifest in a surprising form or from an unexpected direction at a time you wouldn't have predicted. It might appear as such a subtle surprise that you won't even recognize it at first!

If the law of attraction seems a little too "far out" and irrational for you, consider this: there is growing realization and acknowledgment, even in the medical community, that a person's physical body is unquestionably responsive to the power of mind. There are documented cases in which people have been cured, even after science-based doctors denied any chance for recovery. Dr. Joe Dispenza's 2014 book *You Are the Placebo* makes strong arguments that even when there is intervention in the form of sophisticated medical technology – surgery, drugs, or both -- most healing actually occurs because *the patient's mind directs* the his or her body to heal. A science-based intervention may be no more than a catalyst which the mind needs in order to put its healing power into action. Restoring health – even recovering from a "fatal" disease – may be possible simply by adjusting belief systems and daring to envision and imagine new states of renewed health into reality.

Actually, recent scientific research is beginning to verify the reality of the law of attraction. *Biocentrism*, (2010) by R. Lanza and B. Berman, uses quantum mechanics to explain how the "reality" of *everything* we seem to perceive in a world "out there" actually only exists as we perceive it in our minds when we pay attention to it. Without our conscious attention, all of "out there" only exists as energy and intelligence, without form and without time. Dawson Church's 2018 book *Mind to Matter* goes even further. His book is a comprehensive roundup of recent scientific research, which collectively gives compelling evidence proving that the universe responds *on a material level* to whatever you believe. *The Secret* doesn't offer so much hard science to support its claims, but it goes beyond the possibilities that *Mind to Matter* explores. *The Secret* gives persuasive assurance – and examples -- that there is essentially no limit to the scale or volume of the material responses the universe is capable of making.

The law of attraction *does* require more of what some would call faith – intentionally choosing to make a belief or vision part of your reality, even when there's no rational way to explain how it can can be true or how it can happen, and no evidence to suggest that it will. Nevertheless, since choosing to believe costs nothing more than a little effort and risks nothing at all, why not enjoy the fun of believing? Enjoy it the same way you might enjoy a lottery ticket when the jackpot is especially high. Yes, the statistics clearly indicate that your actual chance of winning a lottery is extremely limited, but if you don't even buy a ticket, there's zero chance. However, if you buy a ticket, you know there's at least a tiny chance. Essentially, what you're purchasing is *permission* to enjoy the fun of daring to fully envision, imagine, and hope you'll win! The ticket is your permission to give yourself this freedom, which you might otherwise be reluctant to do. The law of attraction as described in *The Secret* invites you to do this same kind of visualizing and anticipating. However, it doesn't even require the cost of a lottery ticket. It's free! (And it's both real *and* powerful!)

The first corollary, **"Have an attitude of gratitude"** is about appreciating everything positive in your life. No matter how bad your situation may seem, the fact that you're still alive and healthy enough to be reading this book is proof that you haven't given up, so be reassured, you still have potential. That also suggests you probably have more than enough mental capacity – formal education is irrelevant in this -- to accomplish some amazingly wonderful manifestations! That's a lot to be grateful for *already*. Because gratitude is so important and so powerful, I'll repeat the definition given earlier:

"Gratitude is the mental and emotional discipline of noticing and acknowledging the many contributions your life receives from others. As observed earlier, you came into the world as a helpless infant. For the first few months at least, *everything* that sustained your life was a gift. You did nothing to deserve any of it, and you did nothing to make it any of it happen. If you believe that you've pulled yourself up by your bootstraps and "made something of yourself" without any help from anyone, stop to remember that *someone* taught you about the *possibility* of "making something of yourself." Someone taught you to *recognize* opportunities. Someone taught you about the *possibility* of seizing an opportunity. Someone taught you about working hard, or showed you what working hard looks like. Each of us builds our consciousness on a foundation composed of such gifts – mainly gifts of teaching – from others."

Perhaps gratitude doesn't come easily to you. Perhaps you've fallen into a dysfunctional habit such as finding fault, being critical, claiming and defending limitations, or crying the blues about how inadequate your caregivers or parents were, or how poor your family was, or how bad your teachers were. Try thinking about your past this way: The foundation you received as a child – however crude, wobbly, or flawed it may seem when you look back – was inevitably a gift. *Some*one *gave* you every bit of it. You can be grateful for the seeds of goodness that were inevitably included in that gift. Those seeds must have been part of what you received, because this fact cannot be denied: the consciousness you've used to travel your path to the present was *good enough and strong enough* to keep you alive. It serves today as the foundation for where you are *now*. (Otherwise, you'd be somewhere else, and you probably wouldn't be reading this book.) The truth is that you're *here* and *now*. The fact that you've read to this point in this book is proof that you haven't given up. *This* is a wonderful indicator! Be grateful, and celebrate!

**"Don't hesitate"** means, "Don't hold back" while hoping and waiting to see a perfect alignment of the resources and available action steps you think are necessary to bring about what you've envisioned. If you wait for all that, you'll never take the first step. That's not how life works. Making your life happen the way you want it to happen is more like a logger, making his way across a flotilla of logs as they drift slowly downriver to a sawmill. All of the logs are continuously shifting in relation to each other due to hidden currents in the water. As he begins, it would be impossible for the logger to predict exactly which logs he will walk on as he makes his way across. Nevertheless, he begins, confident he will find a way. As he walks along each log, he surveys what's available. He selects the best option, steps onto that log, walks along it, and then selects the *next* best option and steps onto that one. He keeps repeating this sequence until he makes his way all the way across the flotilla. Those rare individuals who accomplish truly extraordinary feats almost never have a complete roadmap to their destination when they begin. Nevertheless, they begin, confident that they will learn what they need to know along the way, and confident the next steps will open before them as they go.

Consider the Wright brothers: In the late 1890's when they started making their winter treks to North Carolina's Outer Banks, they *knew* that they *didn't know* if they would succeed, but they had a *vision*, they *believed,* and they *acted* on their beliefs in spite of much ridicule. (After all, people had been trying to fly for centuries, and had always failed miserably. Every sensible person "knew" it was impossible for people to fly, as surely as everyone had "known" centuries earlier that the earth was the center of the universe. Nevertheless, the Wright brothers left their bicycle shop in Dayton, Ohio, and traveled more than 650 miles by horse and wagon over the Blue Ridge Mountains to Kitty Hawk, North Carolina. There, they *took action* in ways that enabled them to learn the principles of flight, which enabled them to invent the first airplane. They had a vision, they believed, they almost certainly imagined what it would feel like, and they *acted, all* despite the available evidence and conventional wisdom about what was possible. This is how ideas that begin in the imagination can grow to become new realities.

Candace Lightner is another great example. She founded Mothers Against Drunk Drivers (MADD) with no clear idea what she was starting, what she might accomplish, or how. She was simply driven by overwhelming grief and outrage which she experienced when her 13-year-old daughter was struck and killed by a drunk driver. Ms. Lightner went into action with no real plan or vision. She simply kept taking steps as "the next best step" presented itself. Each time she took a step, new steps became possible and available. Eventually, MADD transformed national morals and laws about driving while intoxicated.

Here's another great example: For more than 20 years, Nelson Mandela was locked in prison, unable to be out in public working to end apartheid. All he could do was maintain commitment to his vision, and communicate by hand-written letters from the distance and limitations of a prison cell. In spite of those hardships, he remained deeply, powerfully, and relentlessly committed to his *vision* of life in South Africa *after* apartheid. He continued to *believe*, and continued to *act*. He did all that he could from within his limited circumstances. During all that time, outward appearances gave no indication there would ever be a path forward. Nevertheless, he refused to let extremely limiting, discouraging, and harsh realities compromise his commitment to his vision or destroy his belief. His letters inspired the work of many other activists, and eventually, international pressure led to the downfall of apartheid. Nelson Mandela was not only freed – he went on to become the first black president of South Africa.

Here's another important aspect of the law of attraction: Like gravity, the law of attraction is completely impersonal and neutral. It makes no difference how clearly you understand, and it has no bias toward good or evil. Even Hitler and his minions were employing the law of attraction, though I feel certain they never talked about what they were doing in the terms we're using here. Hitler had a vision. He believed, and persuaded others to believe with him. He could feel the reality he had envisioned, and was shockingly powerful at persuading others to feel with him. That's what so disturbing about videos of his rallies. Hitler was extremely effective in persuading others to see his vision, believe in it, feel it, and then act to make it real. Millions joined him in imagining, believing, feeling, and acting, and together they made the Holocaust real. Whether you stumble into a naïve way of using its power, or learn it articulately and then learn to employ it for creative, healthy, and productive purposes, the law of attraction simply *is*. The law of attraction is the fundamental dynamic of how all societies and civilizations are created, and how they continue to evolve.

In all of these real stories, the path unfolded as the actors stepped into it. Next time you're surrounded by a "wall" of fog, try walking to "the edge" of what you can see. When you get there, that "wall" will have moved out ahead of you, and you'll be able to see – from that *new* location – new possibilities that were absolutely *not visible* to you from the place you started. If you needed to, you could drive to a destination you've never driven to before in the middle of the night. You would probably begin with confidence without pausing to realize that the headlights on your car will never illuminate more than the next 50-60 yards of your journey. Living intentionally is almost never a bright-and-sunny, smooth-and-easy, dry-land affair. More often, it's a whitewater adventure, with waves and currents of energy flowing in all sorts of unpredictable and ever-changing directions. Be thoughtful and strategic, but don't try to plan every detail in advance, and don't wait for complete safety and certainty. Jump in and make the most of the available energy and opportunities. Do your best to figure out how to surf on those waves. That's what makes life an authentic and dramatic adventure, rather than an endurance contest. A soaring bird can't see or understand the air currents that lift it up, but that doesn't stop it from riding those currents into the sky where it can soar!

# Answer to the rabbit-in-a-bottle challenge:

**You get the rabbit out of the bottle the same way you put him in there:**
**You simply *imagine* him out!**

*Don't worry if you failed this challenge. I did too, but then I tried to figure out why. Here's my theory: The riddle originates in fantasy. The first word of instruction is "imagine." At its best, imagination is like dreaming. In dreams, you normally and natural create anything you need or want, just by using your imagination freely. For example, if you're in the middle of a dream and you need a car, you don't get tangled up in strategies for finding a car, paying for a car, making sure it has gas, or any of the other details of owning and using a real car. You simply* dream *a car into the reality of your dream, and then you get in it and drive without even wondering where the car came from. That's the mindset I invited you to enter when my words guided your imagination to create the image of a rabbit in a bottle.*

*After you used your imagination to put an imaginary rabbit into an imaginary bottle, you encountered the "challenge" question. Use of the world "challenge" automatically pulled you back into a "normal reality" mindset. The word "rescue" especially suggests a more normal perspective in which there are undeniable and challenging physical realities and limitations. Because the "challenge question" so strongly suggests it, we very naturally fall back into thinking and operating from within that more limited "normal reality." In that version of reality, there* isn't *any way to rescue the rabbit without damaging the glass or injuring the rabbit.*

*Here's the more important question: How can you escape the subtle but powerful pull of "normal reality?" How can you free yourself from rational captivity and engage the power of your imagination to fly as high and fast and far as your situation requires, or as you desire, regardless of the apparent limitations swirling around you? Reclaiming the power of your imagination — along with intentionally managing your beliefs and developing healthy discipline about spending your attention — may not immediately solve all of your problems, but all three of these can be helpful additions to your other skills for living intentionally and learning to soar!*

*A few beliefs that can help with*

# Deciding

As your belief system becomes more accurately aligned and more in harmony with the fundamental and unalterable realities of living a human life in time and space, and as you develop better disciplines about where and how you spend your attention and time, you'll continue to make decisions about what you will *do* — the actions you will take — to "make your life." There will be new opportunities to consider in new ways. Options you haven't previously imagined will begin to offer themselves. There will be new decisions to make.

Time is an important dimension in all decisions. Some decisions are short-term: "What should I do with this unexpected hour I now have between appointments?" At the other extreme are the longer-term decisions: "Should I buy this house, or continue to rent?" "Should I stay with the job I have, or switch to an entirely different career path?" "Should I marry this person, or just keep dating?" You can probably imagine a wide variety of possible realities you would welcome into your life. The more you reclaim the power of your imagination, the more important it will become to make sound decisions about which possibilities will receive the investments of your attention, time, and energy to make them real.

## Some thoughts on making decisions

Generally speaking, longer-term decisions tend to be the more important ones, but not always. Sometimes, what appears to be a very short-term inconsequential decision leads to a long-term life-shaping result. I was once invited to participate in "de-bugging" a newly built ropes course that my friend Ned had completed as part of his work with challenged youth in a nearby city. At the time he invited me, I was driving 18-wheelers, and never knew when I would be home, so it wasn't until the day before the event that it became clear my participation would even be possible. I got up on the morning of the event and asked myself, "Should I go, or not go? Do I *really* want to do this? It will require a 60-mile drive just to get there and the same return trip home at the end of the day. Haven't I driven enough for this week?" I was almost completely non-committal. Eventually my decision came down to this: "I might as well go, because I don't have anything better to do."

It turned out to be a wonderfully fun day. In fact, I enjoyed it so much that I decided to take Ned out for dinner to thank him. I was happy to include his friend Greg, who had also participated in the day's activities. After a fine steak dinner, the three of us sat and talked for quite a while. As we were starting to make motions toward getting up and leaving, Greg interrupted. He explained that he was starting a new job as director of a camping program that operated out of an Episcopal conference center a couple of hundred miles away. He told me that he had already completed staff interviews and had made his hiring choices. He went on to explain that the job offer letters were already signed and sealed, ready to be mailed. "But," he continued, "I noticed how you handled yourself out there today, and I think I'd rather invite you to be on my staff instead of one of the other people I was planning to hire. Would you be interested?" I was definitely interested. By the time we left the restaurant, I had agreed to drive almost 300 miles the following weekend for a formal interview with a full committee. That interview led to a formal job offer, which I accepted. The second summer I worked for Greg at the camp, I fell in love with a female staff member who eventually became my wife and the mother of my sons. A seemingly casual decision that began as "I might as well go," became a major turning point in my life. If you pause to look closely, you'll probably agree that quite often, decisions that seem relatively inconsequential in the moment unfold to have monumental consequences. Since it's impossible to know in advance which decisions will be most consequential, you might as well stay as relaxed as possible about all of them!

One insight that has really helped me stay relaxed while making decisions is realizing that a true decision is a last-second action. It happens in what I now think of as "the moment of irrevocable action," i.e., the moment in which you take an action that cannot be reversed. You may have boarded the airplane and taken your seat, but until the flight attendants close the door, you can always stand up and walk off the plane. You may have agonized about a difficult situation with a friend, spent hours carefully composing a letter, written the letter, and gotten it ready to mail, but until the moment the door closes on the letter drop box (or you hit the "Send" button on an email,) you can change your mind and reverse your course completely. I refer to such moments as "MIA's" — moments of irrevocable action. Until the final moment of taking irrevocable action, you haven't really *decided* anything. You may have spent hours analyzing, pondering, and developing a *plan* for how you *intend* to decide, but until the MIA actually arrives, new circumstances can always develop, and those new circumstances can lead you to "change your mind" and change your plan. If you make such a change, you haven't really changed a *decision*. You've simply modified your *plan* for what you *intended* to decide.

If a decision seems especially large and important, I find it helpful to identify the MIA early in the process. Being clear about when the when the MIA will occur helps me avoid feelings of anxiety that might arise from not having clarity during the days (weeks, or months) prior to the MIA. I actually don't *need* clarity until the last moment *before* the MIA. I don't actually *need* advance knowledge about which choice will be best or feel most right until the moment of irrevocable action arrives. When I know the MIA, I can stay far more relaxed. I can enjoy the openness, flexibility, and the possible "surprise" aspect of the decision-making process right up until the very last moment.

Often, the MIA is defined by circumstances and agencies beyond your control. For example, those folks who are offering you a job need your answer no later than 5 PM on a particular day. Or, perhaps you're buying a house. To secure the best interest rate offered by the bank, the loan agreement must be signed by 5 PM on a particular date. In other situations, the MIA is not so clearly identified, and you can negotiate. "How soon do you need to know? At what point is it going to become a problem if I haven't given you an answer yet?" And in some situations, you can determine and set the MIA for yourself. If your lease is up and you have to move somewhere, you can set your own deadline for committing to another place. If you own a lot of stuff and moving is going to be a big and complicated affair, you may want to allow two full months after the decision to make all the arrangements and accomplish the move. If you're living simply and two carloads will move everything, you may not need a definite decision until the last day in your current location. Even when you have a clearly established MIA, regardless of how it was established, if your decision becomes so clear that you want to take action sooner, rather than waiting for the defined MIA, you're totally free to go ahead and take irrevocable action. Being clear about an MIA is just a simple way of reframing your decision-making process, but it can be an extremely useful tool.

During the time leading up to an MIA, I like to imagine each possible option as a colored balloon that floats around randomly in the interior holographic world of my consciousness. For simple yes/no decisions, there will only be two balloons, one for "yes" and one for "no." For more complicated decisions, there may be several. As an example, let's imagine I have to replace my car. I'm faced with a decision about what to buy, and hopefully, there are several options I can afford. First, I identify my MIA. For example, I might conclude that delaying the decision beyond a particular date and time will cause transportation issues I'd rather not deal with. Next, I do my research and identify the options that are both affordable and attractive. For each option, I imagine a floating balloon. Sometimes, one will drift in close and attract a lot of my attention. "The SUV is probably the better choice because the fuel mileage will be so much better, and it will be more comfortable on long trips." That option might feel really good and "right" for a few hours, only to drift back out as a different possibility drifts closer and takes its place. "Fuel mileage is important, but since there are so many times when I need to load and haul more than an SUV can handle, the truck is probably a better option." A third option might be, "That little red convertible that has great acceleration and tight cornering would be a lot of fun to own and drive."

Usually, as the MIA draws near, one balloon drifts in closer and lingers, while all the others fade toward the periphery. Whenever I notice that has happened, I realize my choice has become clear. The plan for my decision has solidified on its own, At that point, I am free to go ahead and act, but I am also free to wait and see if any "surprise" options appear, knowing that I can change my mind at any moment right up until the MIA. When I allow this kind of openness for the decision process, many decisions almost seem to "make themselves." One option drifts in close while the others essentially disappear. Conversely, when two or more possibilities refuse to resolve into a single clear choice, I rest easy in the assumption that both options must be essentially equal, and it really won't matter which one I choose. When I find myself in unresolved polarity, I actually anticipate the fun and surprise of seeing which way my intuition will lead me when the MIA arrives.

For the largest scale decisions – like what to do with *your life* – some people feel blessed to have a "calling" – a clear sense that there's some specific work they are "supposed to do," and they enthusiastically embrace it. Others wish they had such a clear-cut calling. They look for one, and may even become despondent if they don't find one. If you long for a "calling," but haven't felt one, consider the possibility that, if you really *do* have a "calling," — not everyone does — yours simply may not be "ripe" yet. If that's the case, your next question becomes, what do you do in the meantime? I believe the most productive way to prepare for clarity and invite your "calling" to arrive sooner rather than later is to go exploring. Listen to your own intuition and preferences. If an activity catches your attention, and it's something you've never done before, find a way to go do it. Don't be concerned about where your exploration might lead or how you might take the next step after that if you like what you experience. Take one step at a time. If the activity you've noticed is too big, too far away, too complicated, or more expensive than you can manage from where you are, find the *next closest* version of it that you *can* do from where you are, and do *that*. Every new experience gives you a new reference point from which to see and understand the world, and from which to know and understand yourself. Somewhere along the path of exploring the activities that catch your interest, the work you are "supposed to do" – if there is such a reality for you – will find you when you're fully ready!

Some people are fortunate – others would say cursed – to have a "calling," that guides their decisions. The example of an artist can be helpful here. A true artist experiences ideas about possible artistic expressions, and those ideas arise from deep within his or her imagination. Here are a few examples:

- A novelist internally hears the dialogue of an unfolding story.
- A poet hears words that make up an especially vivid or subtle way of communicating a feeling.
- The sculptor sees a three-dimensional form inside a block of stone.
- The musician hears the notes of a new and different melody.
- A painter sees a compelling image in his or her imagination.

In each of these situations, if the artist is truly inspired, the idea keeps occurring, keeps bubbling up in the imagination until the artist feels compelled to draw it, paint it, write, or sculpt it. Some artists experience this type of inspiration as more of a burden than a gift. Whatever is coming up in their imagination occurs with such relentless intensity and repetition that they *have* to invest time and resources to give it external expression, just to clear it from their minds and experience a little internal peace. (For some, having a "calling" is almost like a curse, because a "calling" can demand all the artist's resources, leaving him or her in almost continuous material poverty.)

For the rest of us, deciding what to do is a much more practical process. If you're deciding on a career direction, it's a matter of identifying the activities you really enjoy most and figuring out the best way to earn money doing some version of one or more of those. If it's deciding whether to buy a new car or a used car, it's a matter of weighing up-front costs against long-term costs, and adjusting that result with personal preferences. If it's about a job offer, you weigh the advantages and disadvantages of the new job against the advantages and disadvantages of staying with what you've got. (People often limit themselves by preferring "the hell they already know" over the uncertainty of something new and unknown, even though the "something new and unknown" may offer far greater potential.)

When making decisions that will probably have big consequences, it's important to include both head and heart. "Head" is the logical, practical, strategic part of a decision. Analyzing and listing the pros and cons of each possible choice can be helpful. Thinking ahead to the advantages and disadvantages, opportunities and costs, as well as the pleasures and pains you're likely to experience in each possible choice is a more detailed version of the pros and cons. When your lists stop growing and seem to be complete, you compare them to see which path looks more desirable overall.

If you tend to over-analyze, you can work a decision almost endlessly. For every new "advantage" you list, you can always think of one more "disadvantage." The list of advantages continues to grow, but so does the list of disadvantages. You never achieve clarity that one choice is more right for you than the other(s). (I've heard this dynamic referred to as "analysis paralysis.") If you find yourself stuck in this pattern, the problem may be lack of heart. Intellectual analysis is great, but until your heart is involved in the process, it's unlikely any decision will ever *feel* right.

"Heart" is the emotional aspect of deciding. It's at least as important as all the thinking and analysis you do in the "head" part of deciding. With "heart," you listen to your internal emotional responses to the alternatives you've laid out with your analytical thinking processes. Then you consider each possibility to identify the one which puts the biggest smile in your heart and on your face. Conventional advice may tell you to ignore the smile factor: "Be practical. Be strategic. Be smart about it. Think long-term." However, as noted earlier, "conventional wisdom" is not always so wise. Heart and passion are also important, and probably more beneficial than too much analysis.

When I was doing professional work, I led many business teams in comprehensive strategic planning. The process I used included both head and heart, but until the last step, an outside observer would probably conclude that my process was far more analytical, i.e., intellectually oriented. (There's a good reason it's called "strategic" planning.) My process always *began* with heart. I would ask team members to imagine themselves, twenty years ahead in the future, looking at a newspaper's full-page feature article about their team. The article would include glowing accounts of how well the team had worked together and how successful they had been. It would list many wonderful contributions their team had made to their community. It would even include direct quotes from team members talking about how proud they felt to have been part of the team. From that exercise, I asked team members to list the *feelings* – both professional and personal satisfactions – they wanted most from working together.

(This can be a helpful exercise for imagining and envisioning your own most preferred future, too.)

After that feeling–oriented opening activity, I would lead the team through a comprehensive analysis of the professional strengths and weaknesses of the team itself, and a similar analysis of the opportunities and challenges in the environment, both currently and in the foreseeable future. After all the analysis, I would ask the team members to identify, prioritize, and select the elements they most wanted to include in their strategic plan. Finally, the team would brainstorm potential strategies for using their strengths to claim opportunities, and select the one strategy that seemed best. But then I would confront the team members with this challenge: "You've put a lot of time and effort into your analysis, and you've made a tentative final decision. As a final check to be sure you're making the *best* decision, ask yourselves if the plan you've tentatively agreed on will give you the feelings of professional satisfaction and fulfillment you said you want in the opening exercise." I would continue with some version of this warning: "You're about to make a commitment that will dramatically affect your daily work experience over the next several years. It's almost like getting married. You're more likely to *enjoy* the processes and challenges of implementing your strategic plan if the content and outcomes of the plan speak to your heart. You're more likely to *overcome* whatever adversities and setbacks you encounter along the way if there's some strong and heartfelt *feeling* in your commitment. Moreover, you're more likely to be successful in the long run if you have some deeply personal commitment and genuine passion for the path you're choosing. It's usually a good strategy to make sure there's some tingling of excitement and anticipation – some *"sizzle"* –in *whatever* choice you make." I believe all of this guidance for strategic planning in the business world applies just as effectively in personal decisions about what to do with your life. With any big decision, make sure it includes an appropriate balance of "head" and "heart."

Unless you're independently wealthy, one of the biggest, most important, and most immediate versions of deciding what to do is deciding how you will earn the money you need to pay your bills and make your way in the world. To prepare for that decision, you need to spend enough time and do enough exploring to develop clear awareness in five areas:

- activities in which you have natural talent and ability
- activities which you enjoy thinking about, learning about, and doing
- the importance of having autonomy and flexibility in when and how you do your work
- the importance of having opportunities for self-expression in what you do
- the level and "feel" of interpersonal connection you need and want to have with the other people in your work situation

Having clarity in all five of these areas will enable you to evaluate employment opportunities more effectively. You're more likely to be satisfied with your choice when it offers you acceptable opportunities in all five. Finding a job opportunity that gives you all of what you want in all five areas while providing an acceptable income may be a challenge. You may have to look long and hard, and you may have to make some concessions, such as moving to a different city, or committing to a long commute. You may also need to compromise by accepting less than you would prefer in one or more areas. Again, these categories are simply suggestions to help organize your thinking.

# A way of evaluating potential employers

The "interpersonal connection" factor mentioned above is more important than many might suspect, so it's often overlooked when making job choices. In fact, sociological studies have shown that the interpersonal dimension of a person's work experience is often the biggest and most powerful factor in overall job satisfaction. It might be helpful to think about the range of potential employers on a continuum. At one extreme, members of the management team have serious respect and concern for the interpersonal dimension of employees' work experience. These managers place a high priority on making decisions that will keep employees satisfied and loyal, both professionally and interpersonally. At the opposite extreme, members of the management team are focused only on numbers, productivity, and profits. To them, managing the interpersonal dimension of the work environment is mostly a nuisance on which they spend as little attention as possible, and which they would largely prefer to ignore.

Some family businesses are good examples of the first of these two extremes. In the best family businesses, *every* employee is given almost the same level of care, respect, and inclusion that actual family members enjoy. Even if you're not an actual family member, working in this kind of business can feel almost like being adopted into a second family. Unfortunately, family businesses can also be the opposite: Employees who are "not family" may receive far less than equal treatment. If you're considering employment in a family business in which you're not already "family," be careful to evaluate which type of family business it is. It's also important to consider your level of need for interpersonal connection on the job. A family business is more likely to offer this than a large employer that depends primarily on employees with highly developed and refined technical expertise and/or skills.

If you're not already loving the work you're doing currently, dedicate a little bit of your attention to watching for situations and opportunities that can offer more of what you want and/or need. Watch for work opportunities that would consistently offer daily experiences that are richer in terms of the five areas of clarity about yourself mentioned above. Self-employment may also be an option you should consider.

## The importance of open space in your consciousness

If these observations and suggestions about decisions seem foreign to you, perhaps it's because your mind has been so busy for so long that you don't remember how simple things can be. Many people find it almost impossible to sit quietly in a room without any externally provided programming. They have indulged in external programming so consistently for so long that it feels uncomfortable to go without it, even for little while. You may have become addicted to the anesthetic effect of pseudo-drama served up by media, i.e., vicarious experiences based on packaged visions from someone else's imagination. If that describes you, it's time to acknowledge that you may have lost touch with your capacity to experience your authentic *self.* The good news is, you haven't lost access to it. As long as you're alive, there is always a possibility of re-connecting and re-centering in your deepest and most authentic self.

Addiction is challenging. Regardless of which particular sources of external programming you're addicted to – it might be television, internet, video games, mystery novels, shopping ("retail therapy,") magazines, etc. – the more you yield to it, the more you want it, and the more you indulge in it, the more you crave whatever it is you're addicted to. Conversely, the more you can wean yourself by not giving in to the craving so often, the less you need it or want it. For some, going "cold turkey" is the best way. Just stop. Take a page from the AA Big Book. Just quit, and from that point on, your whole battle boils down to the next temptation to indulge. If you can keep winning *that* battle, you've won the war. Weaning yourself from over-indulgence in vicarious realities and/or pseudo-drama can free your mind for much more comfortable and effective decision making processes than you've experienced in the past.

Meditation can be a powerful intentional practice for reclaiming open space in your consciousness. Inspirations and decisions both require "open space" in which they can arise from your deepest authentic self. Without open space, the guidance your deepest self can offer becomes buried in a never-ending cascade of thoughts running through your mind. When your mind is quiet enough to hear it, inner guidance can make decisions much easier. Enter "meditation" as a subject on the "Amazon books" web site and you'll see more than 100,000 results. Clearly, there's no shortage of books on meditation. It's also easy enough to find classes at local educational organizations and alternative healing centers. You can even teach yourself a very simple method using yoga breathing. With a little consistent practice, this simple approach can take you into deep and satisfying meditation:

1. Find a quiet place where you can sit upright in a comfortable position.

2. Extend your neck to place the top of your head in its highest possible position. (This straightens your spine and puts your torso in its best posture for breath and digestion.) Hold your shoulders back, and allow them to relax into a low and broad posture.

3. With your eyes closed, inhale through your nose during a count of 6 seconds (or 6 heartbeats, if you can sense and count your pulse.) Use your abdominal muscles and diaphragm, to slowly and smoothly fill your torso with air. Fill it from the bottom up, by imagining that you're filling a plastic bag with water. (It spreads and fills *out* at the bottom before it fills *up* to the top.)

4. When you've filled your lungs until they're comfortably full, hold that breath for 4 seconds.

5. Then, over a count of 6-8 seconds, exhale through your mouth as slowly and smoothly as possible. This time, imagine your torso like a tube of toothpaste. Use your diaphragm and abdominal muscles to slowly and smoothly "squeeze the tube" starting from the bottom – just above your pubic bone – working your way up to the top of your lungs until the "tube" of your torso is empty.

6. When your lungs are comfortably empty, hold for another count of 4 seconds before returning to Step 3.

Practice following the simple instructions above until your breathing becomes completely smooth and steady, and you are able to keep your thoughts focused only on your breath for longer periods of time. At first, you'll probably encounter what experienced meditators call "monkey mind" – a seemingly endless stream of random thoughts "jumping on stage" to occupy your attention, one after another, like restless monkeys hopping from branch to branch in a tree. This is your mind, urgently trying to fill the empty space you're trying to re-claim. There's no point trying to fight these thoughts. If you resist, the random thoughts will only seem to accelerate and intensify! Just be amused by how many there are, how quickly they occur, and how random they can be. Think of them as clouds. Allow them to occur, and then allow them to float out of sight without any concern or interference from your thinking mind.

If you decide to try this method, don't be dismayed if you find it difficult to inhale or exhale smoothly. Trying to control your breathing intentionally in unaccustomed ways will be an unfamiliar experience for your muscles, so give them time to learn. It will take some practice. Be gentle and patient with yourself. Two minutes of practice will be helpful. Twenty minutes is better. Whatever works for you is right. The more you practice, the more you will find yourself able to keep your mind totally focused on your breath as it moves in out of your body. I usually try to stay in that mode of practicing until I succeed in completing a sequence of five full breaths without being distracted by any random thoughts. (Even after 40 years of practicing, I'm not always able to accomplish that.)

In teaching myself to meditate, I started with this and nothing more, and I just kept practicing. It only took a few weeks to begin feeling beneficial effects, and this simple approach still works for me more than 40 years later. I'm pretty sure it can work for you too, if you give it some practice most every day for several weeks. Of course, there are many methods you can try, and you may need to try several before you find one that feels right to you.

# Making the world a better place

For many of us who came of age in the 1960's and '70's, wanting to "make the world a better place" was an important factor when we were making decisions about what to do with our lives. I'm sure it's still important for many. It can feel good to make this a priority. You'll probably even receive some warm approval from your peers, and maybe even from some of the people you most respect. However, approval from others is not a healthy goal psychologically, nor is it an appropriate substitute for authentic personal success. If you're tempted to get involved in trying to "make the world a better place," it's important to look closely at your motivation. If your choice is driven *in any way* by guilt, there will probably be at least a little tinge of darkness, heaviness, and/or bitterness in every effort you make. If making this choice seems to come with a sense of obligation or responsibility you'd really rather not accommodate, your efforts may not be infused with your fullest passion and heart. To the extent that passion and heart are missing, even your best efforts will likely be less productive and less satisfying than they might have been.

Think carefully about that easy phrase, "making the world a better place." The reality of "the world" is actually the current state of civilization. You can't improve on material, energy, or all the life forms that make up "nature," which is always doing just fine all by itself, except where humans interfere. "Civilization" is the collective manifestation of millions of people using their imaginations with investments of attention, time, energy, hard work, and physical materials to imagine civilizations into realities. The estimated population of the world in 2021 is approximately 7.6 billion people. That "world" you want to "make better" is composed of the collective efforts and investments of *all* those people. Be realistic: How much better do you think you can make it when your part is only 1 in 7,600,000,000?

Robert Pirsig, author of the 1974 cult classic *Zen and the Art of Motorcycle Maintenance* offered some interesting observations about "changing the world" in his sequel, *Lila* (1991.) While making his way on the sidewalks of New York City, Pirsig observed that New York has long been known as one of the most dynamic cities in the world. In New York, almost anything is possible. There, you can discover a truly astonishing array of people, many of whom have created uniquely eccentric realities for themselves. Pirsig also observed that until the late 20th century, even large cities like New York still seemed to be manageable. Smart powerful people could assume positions of leadership and actually seem to be effective at guiding and directing the evolution of their cities in desirable ways. However, Pirsig wondered, perhaps New York has simply become too big, too busy, and too dynamic. In the context of evolution, perhaps large cities have become new life forms, unlike any other life form nature has ever produced before. Maybe a city today is more like a hive, and individual humans are its equivalent of worker bees. The city does not and cannot exist without its citizens. It is dependent on them, and it is made of them, but it's larger and far more complex than any one of them. Trying to control or direct the evolution of a city would be like a single worker bee trying to control and direct the evolution of a hive. If evolution wants to take the hive in a completely new direction -- different from anything life has ever produced before -- evolution will have its way, regardless of the intentions and best efforts of a single worker bee. Your intentions and efforts to "make the world a better place" may not be consistent with nature's intentions for evolution of human life on Planet Earth.

I've concluded that if you really want to "make the world a better place," it's important to start by making sure you truly love whatever you're doing. It should be something that completely "blows your hair back." Oddly enough, a really powerful example of "loving what you do" can be observed almost any Saturday night by watching a mixed martial arts fight on television. If the fighters are evenly matched, it's common for one or both to appear bruised, bloodied, and exhausted when the final bell rings. It's also common to see the two fighters embrace immediately following the final bell. They've just spent at least three five-minute rounds, each going after the other with no other purpose than to physically overwhelm and subdue their opponent. Quite often, their bout has appeared to be an all-out war of mutual aggression, filled with some of the most intense interpersonal physical violence you're likely to see in public anywhere in the world. But cage fighting is structured, sanctioned, and shown on television all over the world as entertainment. When I first saw such an embrace between exhausted fighters, I was flabbergasted. *"What* is going on?" I wondered. After much thought, I realized that an embrace in that situation is a demonstration of mutual respect, admiration, and appreciation. Martial arts fighters are people – yes, women are also involved in this sport – who absolutely *love* the personal discipline of developing their mental and physical capabilities to the sharpest possible edge of their capacity for physical dominance over another person. The only way they can truly measure their progress in this discipline is competition against an opponent who loves the same discipline. When two cage fighters embrace at the end of a match, I believe they're saying to each other, "Thank you for giving me the opportunity to test myself. Thank you for being such a worthy opponent. Only those of us who love mixed martial arts can give each other this unusual gift. I acknowledge and respect your best efforts to overcome my best efforts. Thank you!" If you hope to make the world a better place, be sure you love your way of working at it so much that you'll be able to stay "thank you!" (Even if the most recent rounds have left you bruised, battered, and exhausted.)

In most cases, "making the world a better place" can only work as a successful strategy when it begins by making *your own* little part of the world the absolute best that *your part* can possibly be. If your vision of a "better world" means the world would be more filled with peace, joy, justice, and fulfillment, your most powerful strategy begins by revving up the strongest possible versions of these attributes in yourself. (You can't contribute what you don't have.) If you try to start from anywhere else, all your best efforts – no matter how well intentioned – will be contaminated with your own fundamental discomforts and unhappiness. You'll be trying to contribute peace, but sometimes you may actually be adding to the conflict. You'll be trying to help others be in a state of joy, but if any part of *you* is not joyful, you may sometimes be inadvertently dragging others toward sadness. If you're working for justice, but you're sometimes not fulfilling your own personal commitment to *being* just, others will see your inconsistency. Instead of being moved by your powerful example and message, they'll dismiss you, because they'll see you as a hypocrite. If you're trying to persuade others to seek higher levels of fulfillment, but you don't *seem* fulfilled to your listeners, they'll probably say something like this to themselves: "Why would I follow *that* advice? I don't want to be like *that* person." So, if you insist on trying to "make the world a better place," start with yourself: work on managing your own consciousness so well that it results in a personal presence that is strong enough and attractive enough to be noticed by others. This will greatly improve the likelihood that others will actually pay serious attention to your best efforts. You'll probably enjoy the process more, too.

If you still insist on trying to "make the world a better place," make sure you love your work with the same fierce and passionate love a mixed martial arts fighter brings to his or her work. If you love fighting to protect the environment, or to save the whales, or to oppose bigotry in public office, or to stop the slide toward complete oligarchy – if you love *that* fight the same way a mixed martial artist *loves* going against an opponent in the cage – then by all means, fight the good fight. But if fighting "to make the world a better place" leaves you frustrated by how difficult it is to gain any ground, or depressed about how much remains to be done, or exhausted by long hours and meager rewards, at least give yourself an extended break to seriously contemplate the wisdom of the Tao.

The Tao – pronounced *dow* – is that classic image of two swirling shapes in contrasting colors — yin and yang —each one starting as half of a circle, but tapering to a tip in perfect flowing curves, each making space for its opposite. Each half nests neatly and perfectly against the other to completely fill the larger circle. The Tao is an ancient Chinese symbol for both the apparent polarity and duality of the universe, as well as for the unity and eternal balance of everything in the universe, and of the universe itself. Each half contains a little bit of its opposite at its center: a little circle of dark in the middle of the light, a little circle of light in the middle of the dark.

I once sat in a professor's apartment with a number of other students gathered around. We were listening to a monk who was a visiting guest of the professor. I don't remember the monk's name or his order, but I do remember him saying this: "Whenever you look at or read about a situation, whether you think it's really good or you think it's really bad, remember that you're not seeing the whole picture. Every apparent reality always contains a little bit of its own opposite." I know now he was explaining to us the same deep truth the Tao has always symbolized. The symbol's division of the whole into complementary parts is permanent and eternal, but while that S-shaped dividing line between yin and yang appears in the graphic to be static and unmoving, it actually represents a dynamic relationship that's always shifting. It reminds us that the tide in any situation is always ebbing and flowing in a never-ending cycle. Consider the possibility that whatever success you might achieve in fighting back the darkness will probably be only temporary. Whatever advances the darkness seems to make in extinguishing the light are also likely to be temporary. If your commitment to "make the world a better place" has always felt like a burden that often leaves you feeling dark, disappointed, discouraged, angry, or frustrated, let it go. Or, as Paul McCartney wrote, "Let it be." That balance between light and dark will probably continue to shift back and forth regardless of the all the best and most impassioned efforts of all the people who are trying to "make the world a better place." The Tao suggests that while there may be gradual evolution and change in the particulars, the balance will always endure. Neither side will ever completely overwhelm the other. Remember the possibility expressed in the Tao: everything is always in perfect balance, exactly as it is, no matter how "out of balance" it appears to be in the short term.

## Important final thoughts about "deciding what to do"

Before you make your next significant decision about what you will do, return to page 151 and review the synopsis of *The Secret*. When I first encountered *The Secret*, I thought I was learning about an *additional* activity I could *learn to do.* I perceived it as a new "tool" I could add to my "kit." I thought that *adding* this to my daily discipline would finally make my life much better. Now, I see the law of attraction in a different light: the processes described in *The Secret* are what we're *all* doing *already.* Most of us don't *realize* we're constantly creating our own realities, and consequently, very few of us do it well. In fact, most of us seem to make a chocolate mess of it a lot of the time. Without clear and articulate awareness of what we're doing and how we're doing it, our "envisioning" is intermittent and poorly focused. Our "believing" is contaminated with all kinds of limitations and has no depth or staying power in the face of existing realities. Our "feeling" is anemic at best, because most of us were taught as children to stop using the power of our imaginations. And our actions are too filled with attachment, i.e., intentions to control and direct processes that happen far more smoothly and easily when they are allowed to flow.

We were told to "stop pretending," so, like good children, that's what most of us learned to do: we stopped pretending. In this way, most of us were systematically taught to *abandon* the power of our imaginations. Until Rhonda Byrne came along, very few of us understood and applied what super-achievers have always been trying to tell us about how powerful we can be when we dare to envision, believe, feel, and act our way into new realities. The result is that most of us have never practiced intentionally or learned to focus our efforts effectively. Fortunately, it's never too late. Your ability to create and live into your own version of heaven can start to improve, beginning now, with whatever you decide to do in the next five minutes.

If you'd like to be successful at making your life more fulfilling – at learning to soar -- start with compassion for yourself. If you haven't done as well as you would have liked so far, it's probably because you didn't understand the *possibility* of practicing your focus and improving your aim. But now, with disciplined practice and perseverance, you *can* learn to intentionally manifest a whole lot more of what you *really* want and a whole lot less of all the unpleasantness you don't want.

You actually have a fantastic new reason to celebrate: your capacity to imagine the future you want and live into it has no real limitations. You simply need to become as clear as possible about what you really want and start practicing your ability to use the law of attraction to manifest that reality. There's nothing that can stop you except yourself. Learning to fine-tune your *beliefs*, developing strong disciplines around how you spend your *attention*, and re-claiming the power of your *imagination* are where it all begins. And when you create more open space in your consciousness, decisions will flow more easily.

It's impossible to begin any journey from any starting place other than exactly where you are. If it seems a lot of the time – maybe even *all* of the time – that you're caught in a situation that is totally "dead end" with no options, no resources, and no way out, you may have slipped into believing that you have no choice about deciding what to do. If that's your situation, remember Viktor Frankl's insight: *No one* can *ever* take away your power to choose the *attitude* you bring to your situation. You *can* make different choices about how you live in your current situation and how you play whatever cards you've been dealt.

If your current situation seems difficult and/or full of limitations, it might be helpful to think of it as the stage on which you do "performance art." To understand "performance art," think of "art" as the external manifestation of inspiration that occurs in the imagination of an artist. A painter starts by imagining the idea of a painting, or a sculptor starts by seeing a sculpture in his mind's eye. The painting and the sculpture are physical manifestations that appear later. "Performance art" is the work of any artist who gives public expression to his or her inspiration through an activity or sequence of activities performed in a public way. Singers, musicians, dancers, jugglers, and clowns are all performance artists. You can think of your current situation, with all its limitations, as a public stage where you can begin immediately to perform your art. Simply listen to whatever your imagination has to say about how you can be the best possible version of yourself in that situation, even with all its difficult and limiting challenges. Then, give the most perfect performance you can to that version of yourself in that situation.

You always have the option of choosing to live every part of your life as performance art. No matter how much you are used to thinking of your situation as a hopeless drudgery, you never lose the freedom to change your attitude about it. You can start living in your current circumstances with as much poise and beauty as you can imagine and bring to the situation. You can pretend there is an audience of thousands watching you. You can pretend they see you as a tragic hero, living through unspeakable hardship with epic humility and gentleness. You can pretend that everyone in that audience is *filled* with admiration for how you manage to bring such quiet determination to such awful conditions and circumstances. Your situation might be an abusive relationship, extreme poverty, serious health challenges, or something less extreme – flipping burgers in a dead end job, making "cold calls" over the telephone, or sitting in a noisy and smelly toll booth collecting money from one anonymous driver after another. Whatever your situation, you can use your imagination to transform your reality from feeling like a victim, to feeling like the heroic star in an epic performance. All that's required is a little imagination and some practice in pretending. Even if you only manage to pretend a different version of your life for *10 seconds*, that's a beginning. Later today, maybe you'll be able to manage it for another 10 seconds, or maybe even 15, and tomorrow maybe you'll stretch it out to 20. The more you practice envisioning a better reality, the more real it becomes. If nothing else, no matter how awful and hopeless your situation feels, it costs nothing to try a different attitude about it for a few seconds. If you persevere, you'll be amazed at what can happen. You'll probably discover that you've always had far more power to make your experience better than you ever realized.

Whatever you do, as much as possible, do it *precisely, completely, and exclusively* because it is *exactly* what *you* most authentically *prefer* to do. This is the experience of your self, choosing for *itself*.

Choose as if you'll never be asked to explain or justify your decision to anyone anywhere. Choose it simply and purely because it's what you prefer most for yourself.

Having said that, it's especially helpful to remember that both secular wisdom literature and the teachings of the world's major religions nearly all converge and agree on one important point: A life that includes *service* – being helpful to others by feeding, clothing, sheltering, helping, comforting, nurturing, teaching, affirming, consoling, guiding, encouraging, and/or celebrating – yields some of the most delightful and sublime satisfaction and fulfillment humans can experience. Choosing what to do based on greed, fear, guilt, anger, resentment, jealousy, envy, gluttony, narcissism, or appetites for wealth, power, control, dominance, or revenge usually leads to unpleasant and unsatisfying experiences. In fact, choices based on these motivations – more often than not – lead to really sad and totally unfulfilling experiences of living.

*A few beliefs that can help with*

# Coping –

*(Staying sane and centered in a seemingly insane world)*

As suggested in Chapter 2, unpleasant reactions to anything in your reality nearly always indicate a dissonance in the relationship between one or more elements in your belief system and an apparent source of that dissonance which you perceived to be "out there" in the environment around you. I realize that the following statement expresses an extreme ideal, but consider it carefully. "If your belief system is fine-tuned and running smoothly, you'll be able to remain at peace and continue feeling centered in your own personal version of heaven, regardless of anything that happens *in* the world around you, and regardless of anything that happens *to* you *from* that world around you." As I understand it, this is an accurate way of describing the ideal state of mind that has been espoused by mystics and spiritual visionaries for centuries. The statement doesn't suggest you won't occasionally feel physical pain, emotional sadness, and psychological distress. It simply means you won't suffer. "Suffering" is feeling stuck in a state of mind in which you "wish violently or obsessively that your situation were different from what it is." (David Kelsey, 1975) As already noted, Victor Frankl has written elegantly about our permanent freedom to choose the attitude from which we act and experience. "Suffering" is an experience that's produced by a dysfunctional attitude — a part of your belief system you can definitely change.

Before taking any action to relieve yourself from any discomfort or irritation in your current reality, do your best to think carefully about these strategic questions:

1.  Is trying to change the *source* of my discomfort what I *most* want to do with my attention, time, and efforts? How much of my resources will be required for the effort, and what is the realistic probability of success? Will making that effort be satisfying, regardless of the level of success? If I'm successful at changing the external source, is that change likely to bring me long-term relief?

2.  Would it be better to find some way to distance or insulate myself, making the dissonance less intrusive and easier to ignore? What would those costs be, and how likely is this strategy to bring lasting relief?

3.  Is it possible that making an adjustment in my belief system would be easier, cost less, and be more likely to deliver longer lasting results?

In most cases, option #3 is the best choice. Adjusting a belief can usually enable you to simply *allow* the situation to be the way it is. Understanding *why* it's the way it is can make it easier to *allow* it to be as it is.

# Coping when "bad things happen to good people"

Lots of people struggle repeatedly with this question: "Why do bad things happen to good people?" It's important to realize that this question is based on an assumption, i.e., that a "good person" *should* have good luck, or at least, *better than average* luck, as if "being good" warrants and should produce some sort of reward or protection.

Before we take on this question, let's separate "bad things" into four categories:

1. "Bad things" caused by pure physics
2. "Bad things" that are part of normal processes in nature
3. "Bad things" in which people are contributing factors, even though there's no intent by anyone to cause anything bad to happen to anyone else
4. "Bad things" intentionally inflicted by one person on another. (Interpersonal "bad things.")

# 1. "Bad things" caused by pure physics

Physics is the branch of scientific inquiry that studies the dynamics of energy and matter, and all the effects that occur when they interact. Volcanoes, earthquakes, tsunamis, and severe storms such as tornadoes, hurricanes, and blizzards are all manifestations of the interactions of energy and matter. All can be awe-inspiring, and all can be monumentally destructive to both the natural and man-made environments. All can cause injury and death to any life form in their path. But there is no "bad" intent in any of it. Whether the destructive event is as large and violent as a volcano or tsunami, or as simple as an old dead tree falling in a forest, none of the life forms that might be affected – unless humans are involved -- would ascribe any qualities of "goodness" or "badness" to the event. It would simply be an example of energy and matter, behaving as energy and matter inevitably behave.

The study of physics has identified a handful of "laws" describing the patterns that energy always follows. The second law of thermodynamics is particularly interesting, because it explains a lot about why much of what happens is not nearly so "random" as it may appear at first glance. In non-technical language, this law is sometimes referred to as "entropy." It describes energy's tendency to distribute itself evenly in any material and throughout any dynamic system. Entropy is what causes a cup of hot coffee to lose its heat to the cooler air in the room around it. Just as heat energy always tends to disperse until it is evenly distributed throughout its containing medium, molecules tend to distribute themselves evenly as well. If you put a teaspoon of sugar in that cup of hot coffee, the sugar molecules will eventually distribute themselves evenly through all of the liquid. Stirring helps, but even if you never stirred, this even distribution would eventually happen. In fact, you could put that same single teaspoon of sugar into a 10,000-gallon tank of hot coffee, and without stirring, every single drop in that tank would eventually contain the exact same trace amount of sugar. That's entropy – the tendency toward even distribution.

The more we work against entropy, the more it seems to work against us. If you fill a tank with compressed air, you're abnormally altering the natural random distribution of air molecules. You're crowding them together and abnormally increasing their pressure. For simplicity's sake, you could say the molecules "don't like" being crowded together, so they try hard to "find" additional space where they can return to normal random distribution. If there's a way the tank can leak, some of the molecules will find it and flow out. The greater the pressure, the more likely the tank will leak. A tank that does not leak at 10 pounds per square inch (psi) is much more likely to leak at 1000 psi, because at the higher pressure, the molecules "work harder" to find a way out. The higher pressure "gives them more incentive" to "squeeze through" a smaller opening than they would at the lower pressure. If there's a way molecules *can* escape from this situation, they will.

The leap from that analogy to Murphy's law is simple. When people create a situation that depends on effective control of numerous variables, entropy causes "resistance" in each variable. The elements involved seek a more random arrangement and resist the human efforts to control them. Increasing the number of critical variables is like squeezing more and more air molecules into the pressurized tank. The higher the pressure becomes, the more likely the air molecules will find a way to leak out. The more complex a situation becomes, and the more its success depends on control of numerous variables, the more likely it becomes that entropy will find a way for a variable to thwart its control mechanisms. Hence, Murphy's law: "If anything can go wrong it will." The more complex the human endeavor, the more likely it is that at least one variable will escape control, causing something to "go wrong."

Humans design and construct all sorts of environments, from the simplest village of grass huts, to sprawling cities with high-rise buildings and intricate transportation and distribution systems for the millions of people who live in them. We do our best to make these environments as safe as possible, but our best efforts are often mocked by physics. Entropy is always quietly at work, eventually causing materials to fail, leading to all sorts of "accidents." Structural elements fail for no apparent reason, causing buildings to collapse and bridges to fall down. Gas lines develop leaks, allowing gas to escape into clouds where the slightest spark can trigger an explosion. The materials used in electrical equipment break down, causing the equipment to fail, leading to power failures and catastrophic fires. Entropy is always at work. All of these kinds of failures continue to occur, and *will* continue, in spite of our best efforts to control all the variables.

We also design and build all sorts of machinery and equipment, including millions of cars and trucks. In terms of physics, cars and trucks are multi-ton projectiles moving at high speeds. They manifest tremendous amounts of kinetic energy, and that energy will inevitably obey the laws of physics. We go to great lengths to design and build vehicles that are safe, and roadways that help to ensure that safety. Nevertheless, Murphy is always lurking. I once read about two Baptist ministers traveling Interstate 77 in West Virginia on their way to a church meeting. The driver was following a heavily loaded 18-wheeler. Because of the heavy load, the rubber tires under the trailer were "squirming" – flexing out of shape and back into shape as the flexible rubber interacted with the hard pavement. As one of the tires rolled over a stray piece of scrap metal, the squirming rubber sent the scrap of metal flying up into the air. It crashed through the windshield of the ministers' car and struck the passenger in the neck. He bled to death before medical help could arrive. That accident was caused by random physical forces behaving normally, with no involvement of any "good" or "bad" motivations. Murphy is relentless, and the dynamics of physics are entirely impersonal and neutral.

## 2.  "Bad things" caused by the dynamics of nature

Think of nature as having both a light side and a dark side. Its light side is full of creativity and beauty: flowers, sunsets, the changing of the seasons, pets with amazing "personalities," and newborn babies.

Its dark side is filled with incredible destructiveness. As previously noted, earthquakes, volcanoes, tsunamis, and tornados are all sudden and violent. Others forms of destructiveness are more subtle, but can be even more devastating. Epidemics, for example, can bring quiet but agonizing death to most or even all of a population in a very short time.

"Bad things" happen to animals and plants in nature all the time. If the weather is not favorable, animals starve, die of thirst, or become so weakened by malnutrition and dehydration they become vulnerable to disease and/or parasites. Plants suffer the same fates: the ones that try to grow in poor soil may wither. Not enough rain causes plants to shrivel and die from lack of moisture in the soil. Too much rain can saturate the ground so completely that roots can't breathe, causing plants to drown. Just like animals, plants are subject to health challenges – diseases, infections, and parasites. Also like animals, they are more vulnerable when they've been weakened by malnutrition and/or dehydration. As much as we prefer to see ourselves as different from all the other plant and animal life forms, at the level of pure biology, nature doesn't recognize any differences. Even when we make sure we have adequate nutrition and water, our bodies can fail, and some forms of disease are still able to defeat our immune systems and our best efforts to prevent and cure. A weakened blood vessel in the brain of any animal can burst, causing an aneurysm –internal bleeding that often results in permanent impairment, if not death. The fact that we experience consciousness does not change the fact that our human bodies are physical biological units, subject to all the same dynamics of biology and nature as any other life form in time and space.

The existence of predators can be seen as another example of "bad things in nature." In fact, every level of the food chain depends on the levels below it. All life forms on the lowest level eat plants, or the remains of dead plants and/or dead animals. Many of the other life forms on higher levels make their living – at least in part – by attacking and devouring other animals. When a lion is deciding whether to attack an older and weaker member of the herd or the youngster that's strong but inexperienced, the lion doesn't ask itself any kind of ethical questions about which deserves to live more than the other. The lion's only question is, "Which target is more likely to result in a successful kill?" The youngster's innocence does not register in the lion's calculations. Nature can be beautiful, but it is also filled with impersonal violence and destruction. For all our "specialness," we humans are in no way immune from any of these natural processes. They all happen without any awareness of "good" or "bad." No awareness, no acknowledgment, no deference. We are left to realize that our assessments of "good" and "bad" are value judgments that exist only in our minds. Those judgments have no corollaries out there in the world where supposedly "bad" things happen. There's no meaning, and no explanation, other than the fact that in nature, death and destruction are always in balance with life and creation.

## 3.  "Bad things" caused by people, even when there's no *intention* to cause anything "bad"

The world of human interaction also has both a light and a dark side. On the light side, humans can be exquisitely beautiful, as when people write wonderful music, discover life-changing innovations and inventions, and when they teach, serve, and heal each other with mind-boggling sensitivity and care. On the dark side, humans make mistakes that lead to tragic consequences for others, even though there was never any intention to cause pain, harm, or destruction. The full spectrum of human behavior includes manifestations of both sides.

When "bad things" unintentionally happen to people, we usually call them "accidents." Some are caused by human miscalculations and mistakes. The 1986 Challenger space shuttle disaster is a good example. Post-flight inspections following several earlier shuttle flights had revealed that O-rings, which are part of the external fuel tank assemblies, were being damaged by hot gasses from the burning fuel. According to the safety protocols in place at the time, any damage at all was out of tolerance and should have resulted in immediate grounding of the entire shuttle fleet until an improved design could be tested and verified and improved O-rings could be installed on all fuel tanks. However, a psychological flaw called "normalization of deviance" intervened. That's the name given to a human tendency to ignore danger if previous experiences of ignoring danger have not produced catastrophic results. Normalization of deviance is a form of magical thinking: believing something is true because you want *so much* for it to be true, even when there's clear evidence suggesting it's not true. Previous shuttle flights had experienced dangerous damage to O-rings, but no equipment failures had resulted. So, under extreme political and economic pressure to "ramp up" to 22 shuttle flights per year, engineers ignored their own safety protocols and clear indications of extreme danger. They continued to approve shuttle flights with defective O-rings. Eventual disaster was almost inevitable. There was no intent to cause harm, and good people were trying to do their jobs well, but humans are imperfect. NASA engineers made flawed decisions with catastrophic consequences.

Some accidents are caused by factors as simple as poor communication. On January 25, 1990, an Avianca Boeing 707 was flying from Bogota, Columbia to JFK airport in Queens, New York. Air traffic controllers at JFK directed the pilot into a holding pattern. The pilot knew he was low on fuel, but for reasons that will never be known, he did not declare a "fuel emergency," which would have triggered an entirely different response from the tower. Because he failed to use the required key words "fuel emergency" in his communications, flight controllers failed to understand the urgency of his situation. They continued to instruct the pilot to maintain a holding pattern. When the pilot finally informed flight controllers that he only had five minutes of fuel remaining, he *still* had not declared a "fuel emergency." By that point, however, it was too late. Before the pilot and flight controllers could land the plane safely on the ground, it ran out of fuel and crashed, killing eight of the 9 crew members and 65 of the 149 passengers on board.

Some accidents are caused by neglect or distraction. A driver texting on a cell phone fails to notice a red traffic light. He drives full speed into an intersection and T-bones another vehicle, instantly killing a pregnant mother, her unborn child, and her 3-year old who was riding in the passenger seat. The texting driver had no intention of causing harm to anyone. He simply failed to anticipate all the possible effects of his irresponsible choices. (An insect coming through an open window could just as easily cause a similarly disastrous distraction.)

And of course, there's good old-fashioned irresponsibility. The owner of a car with bald tires doesn't want to spend the money for new ones. He suffers a blowout while driving at high speed. His car veers into oncoming traffic and causes a head-on collision killing an innocent retired couple. A construction supervisor fails to insist on proper safety equipment for his workers. A worker accidentally drops a brick which falls on the unprotected head of a worker below, causing a a serious concussion, a broken neck, and permanent paralysis. A simple hardhat would have made all the difference. Similar accidents occur every day, all over the world. In most of these accidents, no one has any intention of causing harm or damage to anyone. Bad things still happen to all kinds of good people, and bad things happen in equal measure to bad people.

Here's another interesting way of thinking about accidents in which people's actions are the causes, even though there's absolutely no intent to cause harm. In some cases, the reasons are so obscure that no amount of investigation will ever produce a reasonable explanation. Most people have limited awareness of how powerfully they are creating their own realities, so they're not intentional or careful about how they expend their energies. Their intent is often out of focus and their aim is often poor. It's probably safe to assume there's a lot of random creative energy flying around in the environment. The implication is that random creative energy unleashed by naïve individuals sometimes manifests as seemingly unexplainable events that are sometimes catastrophic. Freak accidents can be thought of as corollaries to the processes by which ordinary wind and heat sometimes stir ocean waves into storms that become hurricanes.

Not long ago, I was driving on an interstate when the car ahead of me went completely out of control. It hit a retaining wall, bounced off, and came to a stop sideways in the middle lane directly in front of me. Fortunately, I was able to stop before hitting it. I jumped from my car, and was one of the first to reach the vehicle to see if everyone inside was OK. Aside from being severely "shaken up," none of the vehicle's occupants were injured. However, the driver was almost hysterical, and kept repeating, "I don't understand what happened! One second I was going down the road and everything was fine! The next second, we were completely out of control!" In spite of our best efforts to control all the variables, freak "accidents" still happen for no apparent reason. Sometimes, we're allowed to enjoy the luxury of a logical explanation; other times we're left with questions that can never be answered.

## 4. "Bad things" intentionally inflicted by one person on another

The first three categories of "bad things" are admittedly easier to accommodate than the fourth. However, a sane response to the fourth may be as simple as accepting the fact that there will always be a few severely disturbed individuals – humans with extremely dysfunctional belief systems – committing horrendous acts.

Unfortunately, these events happen many times, every day, in every corner of the earth. People fail to manage their consciousness effectively. Most don't even realize the *possibility* of managing their consciousness. Still, they forge ahead, trusting blindly in the beliefs they were taught – which they dutifully incorporated into their belief systems. They do their best to pursue and obtain the things they believe will bring them happiness and/or a sense of fulfillment. The net result of all this blind thinking, deciding, and grasping, is a world filled with dysfunctional thinking, dysfunctional decisions, and actions that are often as counter-productive for the actors as they are for the victims.

When I see or hear about people intentionally choosing to inflict interpersonal disrespect, animosity, aggression, violation, injury, and/or death on each other, I usually try to remind myself of two assumptions:

1.  A person who makes such choices is almost certainly being dominated by severely unhealthy or damaged ego. This is a useful way to think about what's actully going on when someone is said to be "possessed by the devil." (There's no external devil unless you've decided to pretend one into existence in your own personal reality.) However, it's clearly possible – and it obviously happens frequently – for a damaged ego to take such complete control of a person's motivations that the actions that person chooses are interpersonally and socially disastrous, causing pain and suffering for others. When the external manifestation is horribly twisted, hurtful, and/or destructive, it's safe to assume that the perpetrator's internal life is probably a living hell that's even worse. Outrage, anger, and judgment from you or anyone else may not even register in such a person's internal awareness.

2.  "Everyone is always doing the best they can." Admittedly, this is an extremely idealistic, assumption, but I find it well worth considering. Here's how that assumption makes sense and seems reasonable to me: I find it difficult to imagine that anyone ever starts their day or enters a situation with a willful intention *purely focused* on inflicting pain, injury, or suffering on others. Certainly there *are* people who knowingly inflict

extreme distress. However, I believe that in most cases, the distress they inflict is not their primary intent; it is accepted by the perpetrators as an inevitable side effect, i.e., a collateral damage in the pursuit of some other agenda to which the perpetrators are committed. People who inflict such distress are actually doing the same thing we all do: searching for and seeking their own personal versions of heaven. Unfortunately, the horrors they cause are an overwhelmingly convincing indication that the perpetrators are internally lost and confused -- some might use the term "twisted" -- in their searching. Being lost is usually a frightening experience, and people who live in fear often make choices that look irrational and produce results that are hurtful or destructive in their own lives and/or the lives of others around them.

In his book *People of the Lie*, (1983) psychiatrist Scott Peck defined an "evil" person as one who is so mentally and emotionally disturbed, that he or she actually experiences personal fulfillment and gratification from intentionally inflicting emotional, psychological, and/or physical pain on another person. While Peck admitted that such people *do* exist in the world, he argued that they are extremely rare.

It makes far more sense to assume that anyone who chooses such a course is naively following a line of flawed reasoning. They've concluded that what they're choosing to do is the most appropriate course of action in response to circumstances as they understand them. In their mental processing, they believe their choices are *necessary* to fulfill some agenda or serve some purpose that seems right and important. For example, a man verbally attacks his girlfriend because he believes she was disrespectful to him. In his mind, "getting even" is the only appropriate response, which makes causing emotional pain for the girlfriend a "correct" course of action. A rising business manager sabotages a co-worker to secure a promotion. He *knows* that sabotaging the rival is nasty business — he *knows* it's dishonest and immoral — but he concludes it *must* be done to achieve that "higher" end result of securing the promotion for himself and his family. In most cases where one person seems to intentionally inflict pain on another, there's some version of this kind of flawed reasoning at the heart of the decision. The "flaw" is nearly always to be found in a dysfunctional belief system in the person who commits the acts that cause the pain.

I believe most people who do "bad things" to other people know, on some level, even as they're in the middle of carrying out their actions, that what they're doing is harmful. But because of deep psychological or emotional wounds, a severely damaged or twisted ego that has been left without nurture and healing for far too long, or because they misunderstood events in childhood and mistakenly "learned" to incorporate deeply dysfunctional beliefs into their belief systems, they are incapable of making better decisions and taking better actions. Their dysfunctional beliefs may even cause them as much frustration and pain as they cause for the people who are their victims.

"But what about the rapist or pedophile?" you ask. Admittedly, it can be extremely difficult to stay centered in a peaceful and loving version of your own personal heaven when examples of such horrific interpersonal violation, abuse, and injustice come to your attention. It's easy enough to read an account of such a crime and imagine to yourself, "Surely this person knew how horrendous this would be, even as he was deciding to do it!" And yes, maybe he *did* realize.

Maybe he *knew* how bad it would be as clearly as you do. Maybe he even felt terrible about what he was preparing to do *before* he did it. Maybe he was just as capable of *imagining* a better course of action as you are. However, for unknown reasons, when the moment of action arrived, he was unable to actually *make* that better choice which would have resulted in less hurtful and less destructive actions

You've probably imagined better choices for yourself sometimes. Maybe you've imagined losing weight, switching to a healthier diet, getting more exercise, managing your money more effectively, or not wasting so much time watching television. Did the fact that you could *imagine yourself* making better choices give you everything you needed to actually follow through, *make* better decisions, and *take* better actions?

As part of my belief system, I prefer to assume that "everyone is always doing the best they can." I realize this does nothing to prevent "bad things." It does nothing to right the wrongs, repair the damage, or soothe the pain and suffering of victims. However, it does help me refrain from judging – or in the extreme, hating – those who do "bad things" to each other. It enables me to view them instead with some compassion. It creates a little openness in which to remember that, while judgment and hate are tempting and easy, love is more likely to have healing effects. Sending your love into such situations is not easy. It takes determined effort. Even if you can't see any positive effect of the love you offer, *you* will feel its positive healing effects in your own experience.

Most of this section dealing with "intentionally chosen interpersonal bad things" was written with an intent to offer guidance for dealing with bad behavior on a personal level. It's also important to consider "intentionally chosen interpersonal bad things" that occur on an institutional level. Unfortunately, individuals with extremely dysfunctional belief systems sometimes rise to high levels of institutional power. They are able to enlist the loyalty and best efforts of others in massive programs in which horrendous levels of oppression and violence by one group of players on another group of players is their *core* strategy for winning. Stalin was running this kind of game when he wreaked oppression and extermination on millions of Russian peasants. Hitler persuaded thousands of otherwise reasonable German citizens to participate willingly in his large-scale program of ethnic cleansing, which was based on his disastrously dysfunctional belief about the supposed "superiority" of the Aryan race.

More recently, Pol Pot and Chairman Mao created similar dysfunctional realities in Cambodia and China. All of these men were able to lead entire governments in systematic institutionalized infliction of horrible atrocities on their own citizens. As of this writing, Syrian president Bashar Al-Assad has been bombing and poisoning his own citizens for more than seven years, with an estimated death toll of more than 400,000, not to mention the millions of seriously wounded and displaced, both psychologically and geographically.

Most recently, Donald Trump managed to persuade almost half of American voters to support his disastrous vision of what the United States should be, and he was elected President in 2016. After four years of systematically disparaging and undermining widely respected and time-honored traditions and principles of American government and public life, he ran for re-election. The country barely managed to avoid giving hm a second term, but still suffers the divisive effects of a huge minority of citizens who continue to live in the disrespectful, heartless, and narcissistic belief system Trump promoted. That subset of the American electorate will probably continue to be a threat to the unity of the nation for years to come.

In each case, millions fell under the spell of a single individual who suffered from profoundly dysfunctional beliefs, and together, they willingly participated in creating massively destructive and hurtful realities. All it takes is one seriously dysfunctional belief system in one person who has a powerful capacity to persuade and enlist others.

If sadness and discomfort are always a function of a dissonant relationship between an "external cause" and an element in your belief system, what adjustment to a belief system can enable a caring person to cope, i.e., to stay calm, centered, and able to act constructively in the face of such horror? At the risk of sounding extremely callous, I believe the most appropriate response to this fourth category of "bad things" is the same as the response to the other three categories. You only make misery for yourself if you refuse to acknowledge that "intentionally chosen interpersonal bad things" on an institutional level are part of the repertoire of all possible human choices and behaviors. Any perspective on human living that does not acknowledge and include such potential for horror is simply not accurate or complete. To believe otherwise is simply naïve and unrealistic. When your belief system is out-of-sync with the fundamental realities of human living in time and space, discomfort, frustration, irritation, and/or sadness and will almost inevitably result.

If a bolt of lightning – (pure physics) – killed your best friend, would it make sense to become angry at the sky and spend the rest of your life trying to prevent lightning? Of course not. If your friend died of cancer – (nature) – would it make sense to respond by including the threat of cancer into your normal reality in a much more powerful way? You could focus a lot of attention on it. You could imagine that threat so powerfully into your reality that it could begin to seem like a massive dark cloud – so big, so dark, so wide, that it could make most of your days seem like twilight. You might even spend so much attention on it that you make cancer a reality in your own body. Whether you want it, or don't want it, focusing attention on it makes it more real. Would that be a productive response that would help you live into your own heaven? If your best friend were the one killed by the texting teenage driver – an unintentional bad thing – how much difference could you make, realistically, by trying to change the way adolescents spend their attention?

Horrors will continue to occur at both individual and the institutional levels, just as artists will continue to produce inspired creations of exquisite beauty, and normal everyday people will continue to love and care for each other in millions of tiny unsung ways. *All of that* is the reality of the human experience, including the parts that are most disturbing and most uncomfortable. It has always been that way, and the Tao suggests it probably always will be.

If you still find it almost impossible to cope with "bad things," if you feel overwhelming compelled to *do something* to offset, prevent, or help people heal from a version of "badness" that seems to impinge on your consciousness, you are certainly free to spend your time, attention, and efforts in that response. However, as stated in the previous chapter on Doing, that response is unlikely to help you learn to soar unless what you *experience* in the *process* of doing that work *is its own reward*. If you can do that work, whatever it is, without needing to see a permanent result, if the simple act of *doing it* is fulfilling enough, even if your efforts fail to produce noticeable results, then, by all means, go *do* that work. However, if doing that work would require you to leave behind a life that you'd really rather be living, or if doing that work would leave you feeling unacceptably exhausted and depleted, you might want to re-read "Making the World a Better Place." (p. 181)

As already discussed, the most powerful way to work at "making the world a better place" may be simply making yourself the most beautiful version of yourself you can be. Allowing yourself to become filled with judgment and hate has no place in that strategy. Learning to stay centered in your own personal version of heaven is likely to be more helpful, and it will certainly give you a more peaceful and satisfying experience than allowing yourself to be consumed in anger, judgment, and condemnation.

## Coping with the cacophony of internalized voices

If you're like most people, you probably experience at least four groups of internal voices, speaking inside your consciousness:

1.  Voices which you internalized primarily from caregivers and authorities who presided over your childhood process of growing toward adolescence. Some were healthy and nurturing. Others compromised your belief system with dysfunctional elements. You internalized most of them to some degree without choosing, because you were dependent on them, and you were too young and inexperienced to recognize any distinctions or make better choices.

2. Voices of teachers you began to actively consider, and choose or reject, about the time you emerged from the naïve innocence of childhood into the growing self-awareness of adolescence. Some of these were primary sources -- people you encountered and came to know directly and personally. Others were secondary -- you encountered them in published sources like books, television, and movies.

3. Authoritative and restrictive voices that have invaded your consciousness without invitation. Some may have come from people you've known directly who served as authority figures in your educational processes, or later in your work environment. Still others may have originated in advertising or from public rules, regulations, warnings, etc.

4. Voices from self-narration -- your best efforts to capture lessons from your own experiences.

Although you have one relatively constant physical body and one constant name, it may be useful to think of yourself, not as a single unified and succinct entity, but as a whole group of internal selves, each represented by a unique voice with its own agenda. These voices all speak at various times inside your head, and collectively, they're what you're referring to when you use the term "I." It may be helpful to think of them as members of an internal self-management committee. We all know how dysfunctional a committee can be. Your internal committee is probably no different. Unless you've learned strong facilitation skills, each member may feel free to voice whatever it wants whenever it wants, regardless of what other voices may be saying at the same time. Sometimes the voices even argue with each other, causing you to wish they would all be quiet. Your ability to function effectively with people in your outer world – among friends and family, on the team at work, and in the organizations you belong to such as churches, civic organizations, or athletic teams – depends to a great degree on how well you're managing the various voices that participate in this on-going internal committee meeting. Ideally, it's a pleasant and productive discussion. However, that internal dialogue can also be contentious, hurtful, and unproductive. Those voices inside your head can make you feel horribly conflicted.

When an internal management committee's voices become increasingly argumentative and unproductive a person may turn to alcohol, recreational drugs, or some other form of distraction that provides temporary escape and relief. Unfortunately, these "escapes" often become addictions, which, left unchecked, tend to follow the normal progressive pattern of most addictions toward self-destruction.

## The two voices of ego

Early in childhood, a pair of twin voices usually begins to emerge. These "twins" are the light and dark sides of ego. The role of the light side is to be your internal guide and manager as you make your way into adult life. If a child feels loved, nurtured, supported, encouraged, and protected, this voice emerges easily. If this light side of ego remains healthy and is not eclipsed by its darker twin, it eventually becomes the authentic adult self.

In its mature and healthy form, the authentic adult voice is a characterized by the kinds of personality attributes often held up as ideals by religions as well as contemporary wisdom literature. Ideally, the authentic adult self is strong, positive, and confident.

This is the part of yourself that is capable of knowing – with absolute certainty – that you are good enough, smart enough, and worthy enough to always do, be, and have whatever you choose. This is light ego, the healthy aspect of ego that must find full expression as an adult if you are to experience ultimate success, happiness, fulfillment, and peace, i.e., your own personal version of heaven.

Unfortunately, dark ego is the complete opposite in most ways. While your light ego feels safe and at home in the universe and easily learns empathy and generosity, dark ego is full of fear and greed. It is doubting rather than trusting, and it is completely selfish. It wants all the attention available in every situation and it tends to horde rather than share whatever resources are available. The dark side of ego can be the nemesis of an overall healthy sense of self. Its voice tends to be critical, judgmental, discouraging, and destructive. It doesn't see any good reason to "play well with others," and is not usually accepted, respected, or welcomed socially. It will suggest and encourage feelings of guilt and inadequacy whenever and wherever it possibly can. While the light side of ego emerges as a gentle friend, the dark side appears as an oppressive bully. If left unchecked, dark ego can become what may feel like an evil cellmate in a prison from which there is no escape.

Dark ego can also include the voices of self-judgment and self-condemnation that adults wanted you to hear when they said, "You should be ashamed of yourself." Its voice often insists that you *should* do a lot of things you actually have no interest in doing. It says you *shouldn't* do many of the things your authentic healthy self genuinely *wants* to do. (If you allow yourself to do any of those "forbidden" activities, the dark side of your ego scolds and berates you.) Dark ego is guilt's most enthusiastic cheerleader. And like most cheerleaders, it wants to be the center of attention, always.

Without healthy restraint, the darker side of ego becomes a self-appointed guardian of your social status. It insists that one of the most important factors to consider in any decision is how your decisions will be perceived and judged by others. One of dark ego's most important admonitions is, "Being accepted and 'fitting in' are more important than anything else." It tries to control every decision, promising that if you follow its advice, you'll be much safer, much more successful, and much happier in every area of your life. However, if you look at its patterns closely, you'll realize that while the dark side of your ego regularly promises you everything, it actually delivers nothing. The dark side of ego seeks to enslave the best parts of your best self in service to itself.

Whether the dark side of your ego is a minor nuisance or a domineering nightmare, it's most insidious tactic is that it quietly and relentlessly warns of terrible danger if you don't give it what it wants and protect its position as the central authority in your thoughts and decisions. Dark ego insists that it's more important for you to be right than to be happy, more important to seize every advantage and tempting opportunity than to maintain respect for values and integrity, and more important to hold a grudge or seek revenge than to heal a damaged relationship. All the while, it strongly cautions against *ever* daring to be totally honest with *anyone* about how loud and important its voice has become inside you.

Sadly, whenever you manage to acquire or achieve whatever your dark ego has most recently demanded, you find there is no real satisfaction or lasting fulfillment. Instead, dark ego immediately imposes some *new* assignment – a new accomplishment or acquisition for you to seek – and it always finds a *new* set of words to persuade you that fulfilling *this* demand will *finally* deliver the experience of soaring you most desire. Dark ego promises you heaven, and the price it demands is complete control of your whole life, but what it actually delivers is more like a private hell. Allowing this dark version of ego to be in charge leads to a miserable life of "chasing the proverbial carrot." That carrot always seems to be *right there*, just ahead of you, *oh-so-close*. But dark ego always hides the fact that the carrot is hanging from a stick which dark ego is holding as it rides on your back. No matter how hard you work or how much energy you expend trying to reach that carrot, dark ego will always make sure you never get close enough to enjoy more than an occasional taste that quickly fades. Living in this dynamic is one of the more subtle versions of "hell."

The dark side of your ego *can* be subordinated and rendered far less oppressive. First, it's extremely important to recognize that the negative voice in which it speaks is *not* you. Dark ego is like a parasite which you pretended into reality inside yourself before you were old enough to understand what you were doing. You unknowingly created it because you innocently trusted the teaching and guidance you were being given. Remember, as a young child, your consciousness was extremely vulnerable and inexperienced. You had no frame of reference for distinguishing between good and bad, or healthy and unhealthy. Your survival instincts told you to adopt and believe – pretend into your reality – whatever you were told by the adults you trusted. To the extent that the adults in your early life had not fully subordinated their own dark egos, they inadvertently informed and guided the development of yours, and you innocently learned from them to make dark ego real in your own life. Fortunately, the *real* you never loses its capacity to grow and develop into an authentic adult self that is fully capable of subordinating dark ego and living in full enjoyment of ultimate happiness and fulfillment.

# Antidote to the internal cacophony: Your authentic adult self

Learning to tame the internal cacophony, i.e., learning to lead and manage this internal committee, is essential if you're hoping to soar. Your authentic adult self is the *only* voice that's capable of getting all the other voices to settle down, listen to each other respectfully, and interact constructively. Your authentic adult self always originates in the deepest part of you, from the same source as your intuition and imagination.

The authentic adult self has two important roles: The first is to facilitate the internal committee in a way that makes it possible for *who you truly are* to express itself freely, smoothly, positively, respectfully, and powerfully into the world around you. The second role is to guide and direct your relationships with the world around you. It functions most effectively when you have selected, developed, and integrated a set of belief, disciplines, and skills that are realistically compatible with the fundamental realities and limitations of being human in time and space. This is the essential core and foundation of all positive, healthy, and effective living. Soaring cannot happen until your authentic adult self is effectively managing your consciousness and steering your life.

When the internal committee is not being led by a healthy and authentic adult self, dark ego may seize the opportunity to make the individual less likely to feel "at home" and "at ease" in his or her own skin. Without the active participation of a strong and healthy authentic adult self, dark ego can cause an individual to live in low-grade chronic anxiety, in which nearly all decisions and actions are shadowed, or even largely dominated, by vague fears:

- not *being* good enough
- not *doing* enough of the activities that earn respect, approval, and inclusion from peers
- not *having* enough money, time, food, friends, or opportunities – not enough to survive

Such an individual brings a subtle mood of neediness to all of his or her relationships. Others instinctively feel this, and most tend to shy away from it, leaving the individual in deeper feelings of disconnection, isolation, and loneliness.

By contrast, when the internal committee is in balance and is being led by an authentic adult self, an abundance mentality becomes more likely: "I do enough; I have enough; I am enough; there will always *be* enough." An individual who learns to live primarily from these assumptions and perspectives usually experiences a constant flow of life energy originating from the same source as the imagination. Because vitality is flowing *in* freely and constantly, there is far less chance of depletion. A person who lives in an abundance mentality is able to give more on a sustained level with less danger of becoming depleted. Such people often become well known and well loved, if only for their generosity. People who manage their consciousness well enough to live in this way often make a lasting positive impact on others. They're inspiring folks to read about, and even more inspiring to meet and know in person. Whether you have been privileged to know one or more of them personally, or you've only experienced them indirectly, it quickly becomes clear that these individuals truly enjoy living. Soaring requires a mature and healthy authentic adult self living from a strong, stable, and deeply-grounded center.

Since many people give up, or "settle for less" before claiming this self and learning to speak in its voice, there just aren't as many people along the way to serve as effective teachers and guides. Learning to live from this self requires time, effort, a fair amount of experimentation and failure, and lots of practice. It requires learning and discovering awareness and skills that are not widely taught. Nevertheless, all the selves are more likely to reach fuller capacity and live in calmer stability when the authentic adult self begins to develop early and is actively involved in guiding the continuing development of the other selves.

## Asserting the voice of the authentic adult self

If you have any concern that your authentic adult self is not yet "running the show" – if you sometimes feel overwhelmed by all the other voices – don't despair. It's never too late to assert the authentic adult self and nurture it into its full authority. If you feel a need to do that, I recommend applying the four main steps of the law of attraction, as described earlier in Chapter 4, Imagination:

1. ***Envision*** the reality you seek. Dare to state boldly to yourself (and to the universe in general) that you're tired of creating an internal experience that's filled with critical voices demanding that you live in a confused and conflicted reality. Announce to yourself (and to the universe in general) that your authentic

adult self is now taking charge and transforming your interior dialogue into a much more pleasant and productive discussion.

2. **Dare to *believe*** that it's *already* happening. Simply ignore the fact that you have no evidence – not *yet*, anyway – to support this assertion. Use pure will power to *believe* anyway. Actively visualize the presence and effectiveness of your authentic adult self, not in some undefined "future," but right now, in the present reality you're currently living. Visualize it being part of your *now*.

3. **Dare to practice *feeling*** the way you expect you'll feel when your authentic adult self has *already* subordinated and quieted all the conflicting voices that have been so problematic for so long. (Again, by sheer act of will, ignore the fact that there is no evidence for this – *yet*.) Dare to imagine your way into the reality you most want.

4. **Dare to *act*** the part, even though it feels like "pretending." (It will become more real with practice.) Dare to act *now* exactly as you imagine you *would* act if what you are asking for were *already* fully present and real.

Keep practicing all four steps. Practice so often that it becomes a habit, and you sometimes find yourself practicing when you weren't even aware you were doing it. At that point, what seemed so foreign when you first started will have *become* your reality. This will require will power and perseverance, but neither of those costs anything. They're both always available, simply by choosing them. Success is a matter of wanting a different reality enough to stay focused and continuing to practice until you *imagine* your preferred reality into existence.

As with anything new that you're trying to learn, trying to assert your authentic adult self is probably going to feel awkward at first.

Your sense of it may be uncomfortably vague. You may not feel very confident. You probably won't feel like you're "on top of your game." That's to be expected: relatively speaking, you *are* a "beginner." That means, by definition, your "beginner" skills are unfocused and unrefined. Developing new skills nearly always requires practice. "Not being good at it" can be an uncomfortable mental and emotional space, but it's *always* the starting point for any truly significant learning journey. This is especially true when you want to make changes in how you manage your internal dialogue. Entering and enduring that temporary discomfort is the price of almost all deep and important learning. If that price seems high, consider the alternative of never acquiring this ability. That will help you remember that this price is actually a bargain!

Another important mental preparation is acknowledging – as soon as you begin -- that the process of learning to live powerfully from your authentic adult self will inevitably include some mistakes. It's only realistic and appropriate to anticipate and expect a few mistakes. Remembering that you'll probably make a few errors will enable you to be mentally and emotionally prepared – in advance – in case they happen.

It's also important to realize that if you make a few serious mistakes, some of them may inadvertently cause pain to others. Some of your inadvertent "victims" might be total strangers, but others may be people you know, love, and care about deeply. Either way, if you're committed to learning a new way of being in the world, it's important *at the beginning* to give yourself permission – *in advance* – to make the necessary errors anyway. Along with that permission, you can embrace – in advance – your responsibility to apologize sincerely whenever you feel it would be appropriate.

# Dealing with internalized voices
# of especially difficult people

Before moving on, a little more should be said about dealing with one more category of internalized voices: exceptionally difficult real people you have known personally and directly in your past. Their voices can be positive, negative, or both. If a person in your past was less than loving toward you – if that person inflicted psychological, emotional, or physical pain at a time when you were vulnerable, you probably remember them with pain, anger, or resentment. Such voices may still have the power to arouse feelings of fear and doubt. It's important to recognize these feelings and cast them out of your reality as soon as possible.

You can subdue or eliminate hurtful voices using the same techniques we described earlier for freeing yourself from persistent feelings of unfocused guilt (p. 77,) or a persistent belief that you're not good enough (p. 78.) Remember that your memories of these voices are creations you have pretended into your current reality. Unless those people are still actively present in your life, their voices only exist in your memory. They have no power, other than the power you give them as you continue making them real by continuing to remember them. Your adult self is fully capable of making a clear declaration that you no longer wish to keep making them real, and that you are immediately shifting your creative energy to more healthy and productive alternatives for your future.

Unfortunately, some of the internalized voices from real people you have known in your past may not be so clearly polarized. Some of the people who repeatedly caused you psychological, emotional, or physical pain in the past may have also given you — occasionally

— healthier forms of psychological, emotional, and physical support which you needed and to survive. Along with the moments that were most toxic, there may have been moments of great tenderness and love from these same people. Their internalized voices may cause both positive *and* negative feelings each time you hear them.

If you have internalized voices from people like this in your past, dealing with them can be a serious challenge. Instead of perceiving them from simultaneous but conflicting perspectives, it may be helpful to remind yourself that even your most well-intentioned care givers were almost certainly suffering from their own dysfunctional belief systems, at least to some degree. It may also be helpful to incorporate the following assumption into your belief system: "Everyone is always doing the best they can." (To review the rationale behind this assumption, see Assumption #2 on p. 204.)

One possible strategy for dealing with an internalized voice that is both positive and negative is to emphasize the polarity until the two different aspects seem like two different people from your past. Use the creative power of your imagination to make each polarized aspect so distinct and detailed that you can give each one its own name and unique appearance. Then, use the same strategy on the toxic version as described above for dealing with voices that are entirely toxic.

Altogether, these internalized voices – from childhood caregivers and authorities, from teachers you've encountered as an adult, from sources you've only known vicariously, and from your own internal narration – influence your choices about where you focus your attention. They combine to create an internal discussion which is constantly reminding you who you are, what you should do, and who you should be in nearly every situation. Collectively, they greatly influence your experience of the world around you. Since they only continue as internal creations you have made and sustained, they are entirely subordinate to your power to manage them however you choose.

# Coping with someone you find extremely irritating

I was recently invited to visit in the home of friends for a long holiday weekend. They live in a beautiful home on a large lake, so it was easy to say yes. A couple of days before I was to arrive, my friends told me that both their son and their daughter would also be joining us, and would be bringing their respective partners. "No problem," I thought. "I'm always interested in getting to know new people."

I had met all four of these additional people before, but had never spent any significant time interacting with any of them, and had only met the son-in-law briefly. Soon after we had all arrived and spent a little time together, it became clear that my initial "no problem" response was premature. The son-in-law – let's call him "Nick" – quickly became a *huge* problem for me. After three days of sharing the same social circumstances with him and observing his way of interacting with the rest of the group, I was so irritated that I could hardly stand to be in the same room with him. On the surface, Nick is nice enough – he's a middle-aged professional engineer, and he's probably a little smarter than most folks. He's well spoken, and he knows how to be polite and socially appropriate. However, it seemed like he had a huge blind spot in his self-awareness.

After thinking about it a lot, I concluded that Nick may be one of the most emotionally needy people I've encountered in many years.

He seemed to need constant affirmation, and his primary strategy for obtaining that affirmation was by trying to present himself as an expert in every conversation, regardless of the subject. No matter how much anyone else might know about a topic, Nick nearly always seemed to be trying to create the impression that he had the "inside scoop" on it. The acknowledged experts may be saying this, and the books may tell you that, but Nick would have you believe that *his* version of the story was the *real* truth about what's actually going on in the subject. It seemed like he wanted his listeners to believe that he had "insider" access to details and subtleties of understanding that no one else had. Here's a good example: At one point, I observed Nick trying to talk with our host about local real estate prices. Nick lives several hundred miles away. I'm almost certain this was his first visit to the area. In contrast, my friend has lived in the area for almost twenty years, and has bought and sold real estate there several times. Nevertheless, Nick was doing his best to convince my friend that he was equally knowledgeable about real estate prices in the area. By the time the weekend ended, I was so generally and thoroughly irritated by Nick that I could hardly even look at him long enough to say goodbye.

I try to live by my own advice, so I had to ask myself, "Where was the disconnect between my belief system and Nick's behavior that caused me to feel so irritated?" It didn't take long to figure out the answer. I quickly remembered that there was a time in my younger life when I was probably a little bit like Nick. Years ago, I had already figured out that when I was a child, doing well in school was the behavior that got me the richest affirmations and the most warmth and approval from my parents. Fortunately, academic success was relatively easy for me, because there was no other area in which

I excelled. Being able to contribute the right answer or the most valuable insight became a major source of my positive self-image. Unfortunately, I believe that strategy may have lingered longer than it should have. I can remember times in my 20's, 30's and even into my 40's when I occasionally let "having the right answer" be an important element in the way I wanted to be perceived. It's easy to imagine now that some of my friends and co-workers from those times probably perceived me sometimes in much the same way I had perceived Nick that weekend, although I certainly hope I was never so irritating to them as Nick had been to me.

After thinking about it a little more, I concluded that Nick's way of handling himself triggered memories of times in my past when I had handled myself in similar ways. Those memories felt miserable to me in the present, because in many of those remembered times, I had *been* miserable myself. They were *not* good memories, and I didn't want to be reminded of them. In fact, some of those memories were so excruciating that I could barely tolerate Nick's reminders. It wasn't Nick who was causing my internal dissonance. Nick was just a catalyst. My own mostly-suppressed unpleasant memories of difficult times in my own past were the problem. It was clear I needed to do some work to "heal" those memories by finding a new attitude and perspective from which to remember them. If there's a person who repeatedly "hooks" you into unpleasant emotional responses, chances are good that person is triggering dysfunctional beliefs or painful memories in yourself.

I learned from my weekend with Nick that I had dark memories which needed gentle compassion far more than they needed harsh judgment. I needed to heal those memories by reminding myself that I was always doing the best I could at the time. Back then, I could imagine being better, but I couldn't accomplish it, and it wasn't for lack of trying.

When my memories are fully healed, I should be able to tolerate the next version of "Nick" I encounter with a gracious smile. Someday, I'd like to be old, wise, and powerful enough to gently take a young man like Nick aside, and quietly suggest, "You might find that it's a lot more fun to 'play the student' sometimes than to work so hard at being the 'expert.' When you 'play the student,' you watch and listen a lot more. If you really *do* know more than the other participants in the conversation, you can enjoy knowing that you know something they *don't* know yet, and you can still make your contribution at the end of the conversation. Sometimes, by waiting and listening, you can even learn nuances and subtleties that actually improve what you would have said if you had spoken sooner. Moreover, sometimes you can simply walk away from the conversation without ever making your contribution. One of the nice things about growing older is realizing that it's not always necessary to say everything you know."

In terms of managing my beliefs, Nick's irritations were actually a gift. I had a similar insight recently about a job supervisor from my past. I had blamed him for not standing up to his superiors when they gave us assignments that were impossible to fulfill because some of the critical resources that would have been necessary for success were not being made available. At the time, I despised my supervisor's lack of courage. Years later, after I had resigned from my job in frustration and walked away, I realized that I had also lacked courage through those times. I can see, looking back, that if I had mustered the courage to confront my supervisor directly or go to his manager in a professional way and explain my concerns, there might have been a better outcome than walking away. But I, too, lacked courage. I wasn't mature enough or courageous enough to face that reality in myself, so I blamed him instead. As a result, I resigned and left what was otherwise an excellent job situation. Those memories are painful, but I know the best remedy is healing them by remembering that I was doing the very best I could at the time.

# Coping with a difficult combination of difficult circumstances:

There are many ways reality can feel uncomfortable: a lousy boss, difficult co-workers, not enough money, not enough time, unhappy partner relationship, uncooperative neighbors, not enough fun, etc. I mentioned in the Introduction that I've held almost 60 jobs — roughly equal numbers of both full time and part time positions — since I worked my first gig in 6th grade. I left many of them in frustration. In most of those cases, I was impatient, lacked vision, lost hope, and/or fell into believing it would be easier somewhere else. I've lived through at least three seriously deep depressions in which "just putting one foot in front of the other" was almost more than I could manage. A good friend once told me when I was deep in depression, "Sometimes, you've just got to put your head down and *trudge*." Another time, the same friend advised, "Just do the *next right thing*, no matter how small and insignificant that 'next right thing' might seem." I've been to the edge of suicide twice and looked into the abyss for days at a time before deciding to back away. All of which is to say I've had direct personal experience with circumstances that seemed overwhelmingly negative and therefore hopeless.

If you've spent more than enough time in similarly bad circumstances or a similarly hopeless experience of reality, two concepts that have recently come to my attention are complementary and might be helpful. The first is from Harry Palmer, author of *Living Deliberately* and several other books, as well as the founder of a large self-improvement organization called Stars Edge International. Here's the suggestion I read about in Palmer's writing: If you're in a bad job situation, no matter how mundane, onerous, or tedious the particular tasks may seem, do your very *best* work, always. In dealing with your manager and co-workers, do your best in every interaction to be the kind of employee and co-worker you would want if you were running the business.

It seems to me this advice can be generalized. If you have a difficult situation with your landlord, for example, instead of reacting and getting caught up in antagonism, choose instead to be the most ideal tenant you can imagine. Pay your rent on time every time. Follow whatever rules the landlord has prescribed. Fix little things yourself instead of complaining. If you're in a difficult relationship with your partner or your ex, steer *around* the "same old arguments." Imagine playing your hand a different way. Imagine being firm, clear, and totally respectful in stating what you need, and imagine listening impassively as your partner or your ex tries to rev up that "same old argument." The relationship cannot continue in the "same old way" unless you get sucked into playing your "same old part." Break the cycle by choosing a different path and playing a role that you can at least be proud of, even if it doesn't immediately produce the changes you want or need. Always imagine being the very best version of yourself that you know how to be, and insist on staying in that version of yourself. According to Palmer, the best way to invite better opportunities into your situation is to do and be the very best version of yourself you can manage, no matter how unpleasant or hopeless the particulars of your current situation might seem.

The second concept is the possibility of living your life as performance art (already described in the Chapter 6, Doing.) It boils down to this: as much as possible, live every moment as if a magical king is watching. After watching, if he's positively impressed, he may grant favors. Assume that, to this king, nothing in your past matters at all. All that matters to him is how well you manage to play your part in the next few minutes. (Also assume there is no danger. If he's not favorably impressed, there will be no negative judgment or consequences, so you have absolutely nothing to lose. It's just a magical opportunity with infinitely wonderful potential.) If that were the situation, what consciousness would you bring to your performance? If you knew that this imaginary king had the power to look on your life favorably and intervene on your behalf to make sure the rest of your life unfolds beautifully and abundantly, how would you play your part to demonstrate your worthiness in the most convincing way possible? Trying this approach, this playful bit of improv theater, costs absolutely nothing, other than a little imagination and pretending. You're going to spend the time somehow anyway, so you have nothing to lose. Why not try it? Playing your hand as performance artist can be great fun, and it can be surprisingly satisfying!

The most delightful part of learning to live your life as performance art is that you don't have to work at it for months to see and feel the results. You can start at any moment, including *now*. Imagine the next little step you will take after you put this book down. It may be paying the bills, or starting dinner. It may be mowing the grass, picking up the kids from school, or going to an important meeting with a client or supervisor. Whatever it is, take just a moment to imagine doing it with the personal qualities you would want the imaginary king of the universe to see if he were watching. Then, live your next few minutes *that* way. And do it again the next few minutes after that. You'll be surprised by how good this can feel, even though it's just a simple game of pretend. Then, remember that you can do this with any task or responsibility at any time. You can even make a habit of it, no matter how awful and hopeless the circumstances around you might actually seem. And if Harry Palmer is correct, playing your hand this way will probably help bring about more fruitful opportunities.

# Coping with the possible implosion of civilization

Here in the United States at the beginning of the third decade of the twenty first century, it only takes a few days of following "the news" to find plenty of reasons to believe the future of humanity is doomed. As I write, the covid-19 pandemic is raging worldwide. Climate change is taking us toward higher sea levels, more intense heat waves, longer and more severe droughts, more frequent tornados, and stronger hurricanes and wildfires than anyone has ever seen before. Political strife in many parts of the world is breaking out as sectarian violence and terrorist activity, causing huge migrations that leave thousands of refugees homeless and destitute. The oceans are increasingly awash with discarded plastic, and fish stocks are dwindling. Elephants, rhinos, tigers, and a long list of other species seem to be headed for inevitable extinction. Coral reefs are dying at an alarming rate. Irreplaceable rain forests are being cut down to make room for more pasture land and palm oil plantations. (Palm oil is the primary oil used for cooking French fries; hardly worth the devastation of rain forests.) Meanwhile, in some parts of Africa, cyclical droughts and famines bring unending waves of mass starvation. Many large corporations make ever-larger profits, pay their CEO's obscene amounts of money, and refuse to provide health insurance or financial safety nets for millions of minimum wage employees. The US government refuses to enact any kind of meaningful gun control legislation and rolls back restrictions on environmental regulations at an alarming rate.

In the short term, you have to look really hard to find even a hint of hope in all this. Maybe a longer view is required. In the longer arc of history, all of these conditions can be seen as temporary aberrations in the never-ending balance of yin and yang. Maybe that curving S-shaped line between the two halves of the Tao *is* –always *has been*, and always *will be* – fluttering like a long narrow flag in a permanent breeze – always in motion, but never really going anywhere.

Ironically, managing consciousness at the highest possible level in the face of apocalyptic predictions may be exactly the same process as managing consciousness in the best of times. Continue to fine-tune your belief system to be consistent with evolving reality. This alone will minimize dissonance. Be careful and disciplined about where and how you spend your attention and time. Do your best to envision and live into a reality with all the qualities of the best version of heaven that you can imagine. If you feel called to make a political statement, take a stand, or start working with a movement or organizations that's trying to change things, that may be exactly what you need to do. Just make sure that your involvement doesn't take you out of your own version of heaven. When you lose your internal peace, you've become part of the problem. The fact that difficult times are almost certainly ahead may actually be irrelevant.

In the early '70's, an anthropology grad student in southern California by the name of Carlos Castaneda wrote a series of books in which he told stories about journeying south, into the Sonoran desert of central Mexico. There he supposedly met and studied with a Yaqui Indian shaman, Don Juan Matus. One of Don Juan's teachings was the idea that Death is always lurking just over your shoulder. Don Juan's advice was to use Death as an ally. Use Death's presence, and the undeniable fact that you will inevitably die, as your inspiration for living really well and powerfully in every moment of the present. More recently, Stephen Levine has written a somewhat similar book called *Who Dies: An Investigation of Conscious Living and Conscious Dying* (1986). In this book, Levine makes a compelling case for realizing that our fear of death and our aversion to thinking about death diminish our capacity to embrace the whole of life and live it fully. By choosing instead to become much more aware of death and more accepting of its inevitability, Levine asserts that we can learn to live much more actively and intensely.

Lately, I have chosen to remember that "the news" is a commercial product that's totally dependent on finding and reporting the most destructive, horrific, and disturbing events of each day. I'm quite certain that the negative events which are reported are far less powerful than the unsung collective creativity, beauty, and love being expressed and shared in every second of every day in millions of small acts and gestures between simple ordinary people who care deeply about and for each other. However, these countless acts of caring and kindness are almost never reported in "the news." We tend to forget they are happening all day every day, all around the world. Meanwhile, many of us *pay attention* to the isolated worst as presented by "the news," and with *imagination*, we rev it up into dark pseudo realities. It's far better to develop a discipline of remembering that all around, there's a far *larger* world of smaller and less dramatic events going on, but *these* events are healthier, more creative, and far more beautiful. These represent the best of what we as humans can do and be.

My best efforts to understand clearly what's going on in the world and align my belief system realistically tell me that however the future unfolds, the sanest choice may be to work at living intentionally and living well, but stay relaxed enough to enjoy the ride as much as possible for as long as possible. So I return once again to the Tao. Maybe everything in the universe really *is* always in balance, even though it sometimes *seems* like it's all devolving and deteriorating into destruction and darkness. Maybe there's no need to try to do anything to change the course of any of it. Maybe there's nothing we *could* do that would make any real difference in the long run. Maybe it really is ok to accept it all as "perfect," just the way it is.

# Epilogue

This book is my progress report from the path I've been following since I began learning to escape from rational captivity. It's all the best I've figured out about learning to soar in my own life. Some of what I've written was as new to me when I wrote it as it has been to you as you read it. There are parts I had never thought of before, and relationships I had never recognized. I'm sure there's more that could be said – gaps in my awareness that deserve paragraphs I've not thought to write, strategies that are still to be recognized and seized, perspectives not yet discovered, opportunities to manage consciousness that others would say are obvious. I'm more certain than ever that learning to manage my consciousness *intentionally* is a learning journey that has no end.

In summary, here's what I've figured out and tried to share in this book:

1. Fine tune your belief system, i.e., identify your dysfunctional beliefs and purge them.
2. Develop thoughtful discipline about how you spend your attention and time.
3. Re-claim the power of your imagination.
4. Practice sensible decision making strategies and skills.
5. Learn to cope gracefully.

Don't think of this as an ending. Instead, I suggest and encourage you to think of "right now" as a beginning. If you dare to begin, I believe your own best way of learning to soar will expand before you as you move into it. Making this a discipline will cause new ways of understanding to reveal themselves, and new opportunities for managing your consciousness even more effectively will continue to appear on your path.

In closing, I declare that I choose, intentionally and deliberately, to believe the following:

1. We are *all* born to soar.
2. When we learn to live in proper relationship with it, Life itself will lift us up and carry us wherever we choose to go.
3. Learning to manage your consciousness is how you learn to soar.
4. Managing your consciousness intentionally, all the time, is how you stay airborne.

I invite you to join me in the adventure of living into the reality of these beliefs ever more fully!

If you choose to begin or continue traveling a similar learning journey, I welcome your questions, comments, suggestions, and insights, as well as any stories you might want to share. I don't promise to have answers to all questions, but I'm confident that if we come together in honest searching, one or the other of us will eventually experience an insight, or maybe even an inspiration, and when we share those, we'll both be richer.

To contact me, send emails to: Soaring842@gmail.com

# About the Author

Mark Becker has always been searching for the most extreme possible experiences of fulfillment and freedom. He has . . .

- completed classes at 4 community colleges and 5 major universities, earning both a B.A. and an M.A.
- spent time in 5 different intentional communities
- spent several years driving 18-wheelers all over the continental US
- consulted professionally for nearly 20 years, designing and running projects to improve organizational effectiveness

He is currently retired and living with his partner Victoria Stone in the mountains of southwestern Virginia.

Printed in the United States
By Bookmasters